Unleashing the Power of BI:
Enhancing **DECISION MAKING** through **DATA MANAGEMENT** and **GOVERNANCE**

Unleashing the Power of BI:
Enhancing **DECISION MAKING** through **DATA MANAGEMENT** and **GOVERNANCE**

Daniel Elacqua, MBA, PMP
& Gwen E. Garrison, PhD

Copyright © 2023 Daniel Elacqua and Gwen E. Garrison

All rights reserved. No part of this publication may be reproduced, distributed, or transmitted in any form or by any means, including photocopying, recording, or other electronic or mechanical methods, without the prior written permission of the publisher, except in the case of brief quotations embodied in critical reviews and certain other noncommercial uses permitted by copyright law.

For permission requests, write to the authors at **book@strategico-consultants.com**

ISBN: 978-1-6653-0753-6 - Paperback
ISBN: 978-1-6653-0754-3 - eBook

These ISBNs are the property of BookLogix for the express purpose of sales and distribution of this title. BookLogix is not responsible for the writing, editing, or design/appearance of this book. The content of this book is the property of the copyright holder only. BookLogix does not hold any ownership of the content of this book and is not liable in any way for the materials contained within. The views and opinions expressed in this book are the property of the Author/Copyright holder, and do not necessarily reflect those of BookLogix.

Printed in United States of America
First Edition: 2023

Cover design by Nurí Pazol

This copyright statement is a legal notice that protects the author's intellectual property rights and establishes their ownership over the book. It also indicates that the book cannot be reproduced or distributed without the publisher's written permission, except for specific exceptions outlined by copyright law. The statement includes the publisher's contact information for permission requests and the book's ISBN number for identification. Additionally, it mentions the country where the book was printed, the year of the first edition, and the designer responsible for the cover design.

Suggested Citations for MLA and APA:
Elacqua, Daniel and Gwen E. Garrison. *Unleashing the Power of BI: Enhancing Decision Making through Data Management and Governance*. BookLogix, 2023.

Elacqua, D. and Garrison, G.E. (2023). *Unleashing the Power of BI: Enhancing Decision Making through Data Management and Governance*. BookLogix.

Acknowledgments

We would like to express our deepest gratitude to the numerous individuals who have contributed to the development of this book. Without their support, encouragement, and guidance, this project would not have been possible.

First and foremost, we extend our heartfelt thanks to our colleagues who have nurtured our passion for data management and governance that better supports business intelligence. We are grateful for the opportunities they have given us to grow intellectually and expand our horizons.

We also extend our sincere appreciation to our clients, whose trust and confidence in our abilities have motivated us to deliver our best work. Their collaboration, feedback, and real-world challenges have enriched our understanding of how to understand and apply this content in real world settings. We are grateful for the professional relationships we have built, and we value the support they have shown us throughout our journey.

To the students who have engaged with us in classrooms, workshops, and training sessions, we are deeply indebted. Your enthusiasm, curiosity, and willingness to learn have been a constant source of inspiration. Your questions and discussions have challenged us to refine our ideas and teachings, ultimately enhancing the quality of this book. We hope that the knowledge imparted here will serve as a valuable resource for your ongoing academic and professional pursuits.

We extend our deepest gratitude to the collegial reviewers, Karen Greenwood, Jennifer Rachford, and Nancy LePage, who provided insightful feedback that clarified concepts, improved the tone, and sharpened the content. Additionally, Nurí Pazol provided exceptional graphic design contributions that definitely improved in the book's look and feel. This book truly benefited from their support and generous gift of time.

Lastly, we want to express our deepest gratitude to our families and loved ones for their unwavering support and understanding. Their belief in our abilities, patience during the long hours of writing and research, and encouragement during moments of self-doubt have been instrumental in bringing this book to fruition. We are profoundly grateful for their love and presence in our lives.

In conclusion, we humbly acknowledge and extend our gratitude to all those who have played a role, big or small, in the creation of this book. Your contributions have left an indelible mark on this project, and we are honored to have had the opportunity to work with and learn from each one of you.

Thank you.

Daniel Elacqua and *Gwen E. Garrison*

Contents

Acknowledgments   *i*
Preface   *vi*

Chapter 1   **Why are we writing this book—and for *whom*?**   **1**

    What is Business Intelligence?   1
    Building Good BI Through Collaborative Data Governance   2
    Who are we writing for?   4
    What Should You Take Away   6

Chapter 2   **Why is data governance important?**   **7**

    The Current State of Data   9
    Don't Start at the End   11
    What does data governance mean to your organization?   12
    What do you know about your current data?   12
    How well do you know how your data flows?   13
    Are your data and your policies in agreement?   13

Chapter 3   **The Five Buckets of Effective Data Governance**   **15**

    Data Quality   16
    Data Ecology   16
    Data Privacy & Security   17
    Data Policies, Standards, Processes, and Procedures   17
    Data Handling   18
    Beyond the Buckets of Data Governance   18

Chapter 4   **Data Quality**   **19**

    Improving Data Quality   20
    Challenges to Data Quality   23
    Quality Data Leads to Quality Intelligence   25

Chapter 5　**Data Ecology**　27

    Architecture　28
    Building data hubs and archival storage
        greatly reduces this complexity　29
    Interoperability　29
    Where does the data live?　30
    How It Works　31
    Common Mistakes in Data Ecology　32
    The Benefits of a Healthy Ecology　34

Chapter 6　**Data Privacy and Security**　35

    The Differences Between Data Privacy and Data Security　36
    Data Privacy　36
    Data Security　38
    Data Classification　40
    Human Factors in Data Security　41
    Principles of Good Data Privacy and Security　42
    Safe and Protected Business Intelligence　44

Chapter 7　**Data Policies, Standards, Processes, and Procedures**　45

    Data Governance Policies　45
    Data Standards　46
    Data Processes　47
    Data Procedures　47
    From Policy to Procedure　48
    The Principles of Good Data Policies,
        Standards, Processes, and Procedures　49
    Common Mistakes　50
    A Framework for Better Business Intelligence　51

Chapter 8　**Data Handling**　53

    Data Handling and the Other Buckets　54
    Case Study　57
    Common Mistakes in Data Handling　58
    Getting the Best Results　58

Chapter 9   Data Culture   61

How do workers relate to their data?   62
Building a Sense of Stewardship   62
Deepening Joint Stewardship   64
Building the Culture   65
Can the culture be measured?   67

Chapter 10   Talent Development Within the Organization   69

Critical Data Knowledge and Skills Areas   70
What are organizational data teams?   71
Cultivating Talent   73
Who is creating your business intelligence?   76

Chapter 11   Becoming a Data Governance Champion   77

Build the Data Culture   78
First Improvements   80
What are the goals?   80
Developing the Strategy   81
Create the Data Policies, Standards, Processes,
    and Procedures to Support the Strategy   82
Seeing the Payoff   83

Appendix for Additional Resources and Tools   85

Business Intelligence Tools by Type of Use
    and Organizational Capacity   86
Resources   88

About the Authors   90

Preface

Since we started our careers, the world of data governance has changed dramatically. We don't just mean that Big Data became a buzzword. The whole concept of data means something different now than it did then. Data used to be sterile facts and figures that only a few people in an organization worked with. The "data guys" would provide reports and statistics, and maybe they'd extrapolate some projections, but it was usually done in support of some other larger effort.

Then the world became connected and interconnected. The tools for collecting, storing, processing, and analyzing data got more powerful and cheaper. With so much human interaction and commerce happening online, the ability to record interactions increased exponentially. Not only that, but we gained the ability to capture context around those interactions and purchases. Data is no longer static, it is dynamic, and there is a lot of it. According to Northeastern University, 1.7 MB of data per second is created for every person using the internet. If we printed this out, this is the equivalent of 60 double-sided pages that are being collected each second about each individual on the internet. Some of it is created and used by nonprofit organizations.

> ## What is Big Data?
> According to Gartner in their *Information Technology Glossary*:
> "Big data is high-volume, high-velocity and/or high-variety information assets that demand cost-effective, innovative forms of information processing that enable enhanced insight, decision making, and process automation."

The ultimate goal of Big Data is to drive profitability from all the collections of data from the users. The only way to "see" the possibility is to create the necessary business intelligence (BI) platforms and workflows. Business intelligence is the story that your data tells. It's the dashboards and the marketing analysis and the future projections that let you make business decisions with confidence.

At this point, we should define what exactly we mean by Big Data.[2] It is one of those terms that has a very specific meaning to professionals working

---

[1]. https://www.gartner.com/en/information-technology/glossary/big-data

within a field, and a more general layperson's definition that has entered the common vocabulary.

Using the formal definition, data generated at high volume, variety, and velocity, Big Data is most seen in industry, eCommerce, and social media. These entities have made huge investments in managing this data, using it to develop things like targeted marketing campaigns built on sophisticated and granular customer models.

Outside of this realm, Big Data more commonly refers to a sizable increase in the volume and variety of available data, but without the big increase in velocity. Nonprofits and similar organizations have the tools to collect and store more data than ever before. But with more modest budgets, they're not able to analyze it to the degree that commerce and industry can. As a result, many organizations end up hoarding a lot of data, investing in storage without gleaning usable insights from it.

Another challenge for organizations is that the nature of their interactions with their members doesn't create a high velocity of incoming data. The lower velocity of data is a double-edged sword for these organizations. While they don't need to deal with a constant firehose of data coming at them, they have fewer data points over time, which limits their ability to identify trends and extrapolate high-quality predictions.

To assess what all this means outside of industry, take a look at customer relationship management. In the 20th century, an organization might have been able to count its customers, tell you their ages and where they live, and maybe throw in a few more demographic details. Coming into the third decade of the 21st century—and the advent of dedicated CRM platforms—an organization has a lot more information about its customers. If used properly, these platforms can give an organization a more holistic view of their customers. Databases no longer contain just names, addresses, and dates of birth. Databases can describe who your customers are, what they care about, what motivates them, what they want and need out of the organization, and the best way to reach them.

But if it's not properly managed, Big Data can be a big problem.

As we have worked with associations, we've found some common themes in their relationships to their data. It's unorganized, disconnected, confusing, and inaccurate. Organizations invest in software packages and hardware upgrades—as well as the staff to support them—only to find that the promises of brilliant insights and visionary predictions simply aren't materializing. This is because the data itself that is driving the business intelligence isn't up to the task.

But there's more at risk with Big Data than just poor-quality business intelligence. There are legal requirements and ethical concerns around member privacy and data security as we collect more information about people and their behaviors. Nobody wants to be in a courtroom or on the news because they had a data breach or used data inappropriately. Good data governance helps you manage your data properly.

We both work with non-profit organizations because we care deeply about the world around us and the people in it. We work closely with these organizations on making the best possible use of their data because we want them to be successful. And in that time, we've realized that we're seeing the same issues in so many organizations because they lack solid data governance. The problem isn't that there is insufficient data out there, or that the data itself isn't good. The challenge is that our community hasn't yet developed the practices and culture needed to effectively manage it. Fortunately, good data governance can help organizations make better use of the tools and data they currently have, as well as set them up to make the most of new technologies that are on the horizon.

And that's why this book is in your hands today. We want to introduce you to what data governance is, show you how valuable it is, and get you started on building a culture of data stewardship for your organization.

Daniel Elacqua, MBA, PMP
Founding Partner and CIO Consultant
STRATEGICO CONSULTANTS, LLC

Gwen E. Garrison, PhD
Founder and Principle Data Strategist
HIGH SIERRA INSIGHTS

Clinical Professor
CLAREMONT GRADUATE UNIVERSITY

CHAPTER 1
Why are we writing this book—and for *whom*?

Before we roll up our sleeves and really dig into data governance, it's important to understand why we are writing this book, and who we're writing it for.

Both of us have worked with several organizations and have seen some common threads when it comes to their use of data. Most of these organizations have some form of data governance but it is insufficient as they move through technology changes including harnessing their data for better decision making.

What is Business Intelligence?

While this book mainly focuses on data governance, it's important to also look at business intelligence, as that's where most people in an organization actually see data.

Most decision makers interact with data in the form of business intelligence. When we think of business intelligence, though, we typically think about a dashboard. Rather, business intelligence refers to using data to tell a story about the organization's products, services, or customers. In other words, business intelligence isn't just dashboards. It includes the process that creates the dashboard. Business intelligence drives the business implications from the data, which is then used to drive decision making. To use business intelligence best, you first need to identify what questions you want to answer, and then determine where in the data you can find the answers to each question.

> ### What is Business Intelligence?
> In "Measuring the Success of Changes to Existing Business Intelligence Solutions to Improve Business Intelligence Reporting," Nedim Dedić and Clare Stanier define business intelligence as, "The strategies and technologies used by enterprises for the data analysis and management of business information."[2]

2. `https://inria.hal.science/hal-01630541/document`

Business intelligence exists because there is no way for the human mind to comprehend the massive data sets that Big Data works with. We need intermediate processes to analyze and contextualize the data to identify structures, patterns, and trends. The next step is often some form of data or information visualization, where easily comprehensible graphic or visual representations of the data are created.

Common forms of business intelligence include dashboards, metrics, benchmarks, and analytics. These are the data stories that managers and executives use to monitor the health of the organization, measure the progress of different initiatives, and chart their course into the future. When done well, with reliable data in the background, business intelligence lets an organization base its decision making on measurable and verifiable facts. Good data visualization can create extremely compelling narratives that allow an organization to move forward with confidence.

However, if the data itself is poor-quality or unreliable, the resulting business intelligence will be as well. A powerful visual representation of bad data can lead to disastrous decision making. The purpose of this book is to make sure that data is consistent and complete, leading to excellent business intelligence to drive bold, competent decision making.

Building Good BI Through Collaborative Data Governance

Both IT and Business partners come into the Data Governance discussion thinking they are living in different parts of the planet—a lot of IT directors are "keep the lights on" people, while Business leadership is often concerned with storytelling. But when start collaborating with our clients and getting their tech and business partners together, they realize that they are not so far apart. There is movement towards better cooperation and awareness from both sides, and this book looks to help them find a common middle ground.

This sense of separation comes about because many organizations place the responsibility for data management and governance primarily on IT. Unless there is a cohesive data governance structure that involves the entire organization, IT tends to focus primarily on the technology and talent needed to collect and process data. Without a strong sense of the business intelligence goals and an understanding of what the data means, there is a limit to what IT can deliver. The best business intelligence will come from strong collaboration between IT and the business.

This illustration shows where a lot of organizations we've worked with have started, and where we got them to.

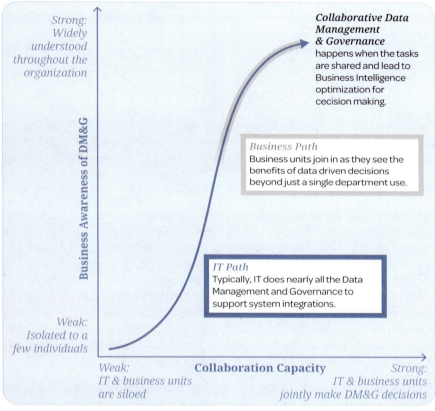

FIGURE 1 *Diagram of the BI Journey from the Business and IT Paths*

The diagram above shows a typical BI journey, with many organizations starting from a place of IT-driven solutions and progressing toward greater partnership across functional units and stakeholders. Organization-wide awareness of data management principles, and collaboration between IT and business, are the hallmarks of robust BI.

There are two good paths that lead from a low to a high collaboration environment, either building data management and governance in IT and then strengthening engagement with the business, or the business developing strong data management and governance and increasing their engagement with IT. Which path to take depends on the organizational culture and the capacities of IT and the business to drive the data management and governance effort.

Who are we writing for?

This book was written with decision makers in mind, not only at the executive leadership level, but at the management level as well. Anybody in an organization making business decisions is increasingly reliant on business intelligence, and by extension, data governance makes that intelligence accurate and reliable.

We are writing this book for those that have both strategy and implementation roles for the organization, chiefly the executive leadership team. They drive the organization's culture and management style. The CEO's values and philosophies are reflected at all levels of the organizational chart. A CEO that is a champion of data stewardship is going to drive a culture of data stewardship. A CEO that doesn't care about data governance is going to have an organization that constantly struggles with bad data.

The role of data in executive decision making has changed drastically in the past few decades. In the past, leaders have relied on their own experience and intuition to make and execute decisions. Now that organizations have access to so much data and business intelligence, there is pressure on CEOs to use it instead of their gut instincts in decision making. This means they need quicker, more robust data in a way they can understand it. A CEO with a good understanding of data governance is going to know that the dashboards and reports they use to drive their decision making depend on good business intelligence, which is dependent on good data. With an informed and critical eye, this CEO is going to carefully look at the data stories they're told.

The next audience to consider is the rest of the C-Suite. While the CEO is the executive leader of the organization, there are many other leaders that are experts in different realms of corporate governance who are responsible for decision making. Many of these executives get data stories targeted specifically for them — The Chief Financial Officer and Chief Operating Officer, for example, have very specific data needs.

The Chief Information Officer has a unique role, since a lot of the work of collecting and analyzing data occurs within their area. Another thing to consider with the CIO is that historically, data has been considered an "IT thing." The business would throw data over the wall to IT and expect useful business intelligence to be sent back. As a result, IT often considers itself the owners of the data. What you'll see later in this book is that good data governance is everybody's job. Business and IT both need to learn to recognize each other as equal partners in data stewardship.

Moving from the executive leadership level, there are the managers that are entrusted with business decisions. While they do not make grand strategic decisions for the organization, they are the ones that take the executive leadership's vision and make it work. Much like the executive leadership, they consume business intelligence and use it to make data-driven decisions for their areas. Unlike the executive leadership, these managers are much closer to the data itself, often overseeing the collection, storage, and processing of it. A good understanding of data governance at this level is critical for an organization because these are the people who oversee things like the actual policies and procedures, the IT infrastructure, and the acquisition and development of the talent that supports it all.

The last audience are the data managers that may not be formally trained in the role. This can include internal database managers, analysts, and other storytellers. In a lot of organizations, especially those that place a high value on cultivating and retaining talent, data managers may have started their careers in a technical role such as a database administrator, software engineer, or system architect. Based on their technical knowledge and drive, they may have been promoted into roles where they are responsible for the data itself, not just the systems that support the data. This audience would benefit from a wider understanding of the role of the business in data governance.

What Should You Take Away

Our goal isn't just to explain what data governance is, but also to help organizations take the first steps towards building their own data stewardship cultures.

That foundation still starts with understanding what effective data governance is. We've broken it down into five buckets that each cover a different aspect of how an organization views or interacts with its data. An organizational data culture ties it all together and makes everybody a data steward.

With that knowledge, we can look at how data governance strengthens business intelligence efforts and makes them more valuable. Most associations are using business intelligence of some sort. There are a lot of commercially available, high-quality tools on the market. There is also an excellent talent pool of bright people that are experts in using these tools. Where most organizations fall short, however, is in the data governance which ensures their business intelligence is using the best possible data.

Between the foundations in the upcoming chapters, and their supporting case studies, you should be able to look at your own organization's data governance. Whether you already have a formal data governance practice or not, an examination of how your data is managed is the first step in building a data stewardship culture. That will help you make the most out of your business intelligence and drive your organization to success.

CHAPTER 2
Why is data governance important?

Even though most organizations are working at a level well below that of Big Data, they can still gain tremendous benefits from the increased volume and variety of data that's currently available. Can a small organization of less than a hundred employees and five thousand members achieve the kinds of powerful predictive analytics that a major retailer or social media platform can? No. But can they still get quality, dynamic dashboards and sharp, targeted forecasts that can drive confident data-driven decision making? Yes, they can. If they have good data governance.

Part of the reason that smaller entities haven't been able to derive the benefits they were hoping for from the transformation of data isn't that the capacity is lacking, it's that they haven't built the kinds of data ecospheres[3] necessary to take full advantage of the available data and business intelligence tools.

The benefits of data governance don't apply exclusively to an organization's current data ecosphere, though. The capacity to collect data, and the tools to use it, are continuously improving. Having very intentional, forward-looking data policies and standards will naturally provide better data for today's and tomorrow's tools. An organization with a holistic understanding of its data will do a better job of implementing new data tools with existing systems because it understands where all the data comes from and how the pieces all relate to each other. Not only that, but an organization with a culture of data stewardship where everybody is invested in the integrity of the data is one where the people who work closest to the data are always asking what they can do with it, and how they can do it better.

Another benefit of data governance is the potential to integrate older data collected prior to good data governance being implemented. This older data may not be up to the same standards of quality and integrity as the

---

3. Term: *Data Ecosphere*. This is the complete picture of your organization's data — not only where the data is stored, but also the systems that collect, analyze, and turn it into business intelligence. The Data Ecosphere is made of several interconnected Data Ecosystems, which is a set of related data and the systems that support it.

newer data. With good governance, it can be revisited, cleaned up, and critically examined to determine what realistic value it has.

This could be used to show how an organization has been able to adapt to social and cultural changes. By analyzing historical membership data, the organization can determine who has been promoted into leadership positions in the past and who hasn't. Younger generations place a very high value on representation, especially among populations that have been marginalized in the mainstream. Ensuring that previously invisible members are moving into positions of influence can significantly help in attracting and retaining the younger members that will ensure the organization's future.

Another challenge for associations, non-profits, and other smaller organizations is that the environment they are operating in is changing rapidly. In the United States, about 10,000 people per day can leave the workforce and retire. Not only are they taking a lot of institutional memory with them, but also a specific type of work style. As they're being replaced, organizations must find ways to make sure their knowledge is carried forward and adapt to an emerging workforce that has very different views on the work/life balance.

The only way to keep up with these kinds of societal changes and grow is to have accurate, responsive data-driven decision making, with good data governance as its foundation.

The Current State of Data

A lot of organizations have taken full advantage of the advances in data collection and storage. The move towards electronic data storage decades ago represented a sea change in how data is managed. Even what we'd consider old tech now, like magnetic tapes and refrigerator-sized hard drives, drastically reduced the amount of physical space data storage took up. An even bigger benefit of electronic storage came from its ability to retrieve data. As data was entered into the system, metadata[1] was attached to it to make it easier to search and retrieve. It didn't take long for people to realize that the metadata itself had value.

One very important thing to consider about metadata is that the business determines the definitions of it, not IT. While the technical partners may be experts in the systems that handle data, the business is the expert in what the data itself means. This is an example of where the business must be an equal partner with IT when it comes to data governance.

What will tomorrow's organizations look like?

Do associations as they exist today have a place in the future? There is increasing pressure in their space from corporations and other larger entities that can use their bigger budgets to draw members and talent away. For example, Anthology is a for-profit industry leader that is seriously disrupting the EdTech space that used to be almost exclusively the realm of academics and faculty. Many organizations are already having to consolidate to pool resources and membership to compete. One thing that is certain, organizations will need to rethink how they do business and engage with members to remain viable over the next several years.

Electronic storage continues to get cheaper, to the point where cost is no longer a limiting factor in deciding what data to collect and store. As more sophisticated business intelligence and data visualization tools become available and everybody is gushing about the possibilities of Big Data, organizations have started gathering as much as they possibly can. The reason for all of this intensive data collection is to make better decisions. Being able to support business decisions with empirical evidence and hard numbers is one of the promises of the Big Data revolution. Organizations should no longer have

---

1. Term: *Metadata*. According to DataVersity, at its most basic metadata can be described as small amounts of data used to identify larger data packages. Metadata is an abbreviated description that allows search engines to find the requested information.
Its primary purpose is to help find and retrieve data.
https://www.dataversity.net/advances-in-metadata-management

to guess at the best course of action or rely on gut instincts. Instead, they want to put a lot of data into a tool and get a clear roadmap out of it.

> ### The Data You Don't Control
>
> There are several data concerns around using apps or systems provided by third parties. The biggest is security of the data. The organization needs to know who all has access to the data, and what kind of security is in place to protect it from bad actors or accidental release. A data breach can be extremely costly in terms of both money and reputation. Another consideration is the quality and reliability of the data collected, and whether or not it's useful to the organization.

Unfortunately, the business intelligence process is not that simple. Most organizations either had no working data governance at the time they started ramping up their data collection, or their governance wasn't keeping pace with their newfound capacities for collecting and storing data.

Business intelligence and data visualization tools are highly dependent on clean, consistent, quality data coming in. When an organization starts stockpiling data without having a clear vison of what they want out of that data, they're not providing good inputs for those tools.

The changing relationship with data goes beyond its sheer volume; the mechanisms and protocols for collecting it have also changed. There is a lot of technology in an organization's day-to-day workspace that needs to be considered from a data governance standpoint. How many organizations have a dedicated social media team and are using popular payment apps to collect dues or donations? What is interesting about them is that they are part of the big paradigm shift in how data is collected and used. At one time, IT was the primary owner of the tools that collect and store data. These kinds of apps put the ownership of that data management directly into the hands of the business.

As a result of all these changes, a lot of organizations end up hoarding data. They're sitting on massive amounts of it, not sure what to do with it or how to make it usable. Even though storage is cheap these days, it isn't free. So haphazardly collecting it without the capacity to gain any value out of it is just a waste of money and effort.

Don't Start at the End

Many organizations don't differentiate between data and business intelligence. Data is raw information, the basic facts that are captured in our systems. The first step in BI work is to establish and create the relationships between the different data elements. We call this analysis. Then, the next step is to create the meaning that comes from the connection or what we can interpret. Finally, when we add the impact or implications of the interpretation to the business setting, we create the BI value. This is the process by which meaning is derived from the data; in short, it is the story that the data tells.

When that difference isn't clearly understood, organizations tend to focus solely on business intelligence because it is the visible, tangible output of the process. They invest in the tools to process the information, and they often put a lot of faith in the outputs without ensuring the data at its foundation is solid.

Most modern business intelligence tools provide excellent data visualization in the form of slick, attractive dashboards. Many of them are quite user-friendly, allowing people without any formal education in data analysis or management to run queries and get flashy graphics to put in front of directors and executives. A lot of tools even come with canned report templates.

With these kinds of dashboarding tools at hand, it's easy to think that a few key performance indicators and metrics and trending reports tell a complete data story. A membership report that shows growth trends and can be sliced to show demographic differences is fine, but what question is it answering? If that report is relevant to the organization's current needs, is it presenting the data in a way that actually answers the question at hand? Is the business intelligence even providing an accurate picture of what the data says? These are the kinds of questions organizations need to consider when building dashboards.

How many databases store that?

A lot of systems and applications are designed to collect and store data as part of their normal processes. This presents a challenge when multiple applications are collecting the same or similar data. At a minimum, an organization has the expense of storing large amounts of redundant information. Bigger problems come in when the data between systems is out of sync or when they start interfering with each other. Databases can become corrupted with duplicate or inaccurate data, and resources can be tied up on audits and reconciliation. Good data governance ensures an organization can integrate their systems to minimize redundancy and ensure any unavoidable duplications are kept in sync.

Good business intelligence is a lot more involved than just picking a template and figuring out which fields to query. The best business intelligence comes from an ongoing process of looking at the organization's goals and challenges and making sure that the data stories are addressing them directly. Instead of starting with a metric, though, you think you should be tracking, the organization should be asking what decision points it is facing, and what data is needed to help make those decisions.

This brings us back to data governance. A strong organizational data culture means that everybody involved in decision making processes understands that quality data is an invaluable asset. The available data is robust and clean, it is cataloged and defined, and methods are in place to be sure that new sources of data are integrated smoothly into existing databases.

A combination of clearly defined questions and good data lets the business intelligence tools tell great data stories that leaders can use to make confident decisions.

What does data governance mean to your organization?

At this point, it's good to take a look at what data governance means to your organization. Taking an honest look at where you're at will help you find out where you're doing well and where you could improve as we get deeper into data governance principles and practices.

A comprehensive audit isn't needed but there are three high-level questions to ask about what you already have in place:

What do you know about your current data?

Knowing what data you have is absolutely critical to effective data governance. This doesn't mean that there is one person or department that knows the contents of every database. With the high volume of data available these days, even a small organization would have a very hard time creating a granular inventory like that. This is more about knowing the types of information your organization collects and where it comes from. Even with a general overview at this level, an organization can determine precisely where there are gaps or duplication in its data collection, consider the reliability of its data sources, and identify key fields that can be used to keep different databases in sync.

Another important consideration in knowing your data is understanding what methods are in place to avoid, identify, and address issues. Any time data changes, including when it is initially collected, archived, or deleted, errors can occur. An organization must have safeguards against data being incorrectly altered. It also needs to be able to audit data for accuracy and completeness and to correct any issues that arise.

How well do you know how your data flows?

Any organization's data ecosphere is a living, responsive entity, making it virtually impossible to draw a simple map of all of it. In a healthy data governance culture, the organization should be able to identify the systems and applications that collect, store, share, and process data. This type of map needs to be actively maintained so it can be referred to whenever data needs change, or modifications are made to any of the involved systems and applications.

The goal here is to understand what an organization's current data is. Having a master catalog of exactly which pieces of data are exchanged between which systems would be a monumental undertaking with little practical benefit. However, having a good picture of what kinds of information different systems exchange and process lets the organization know what the connections are and can help identify potential impacts of changes within different data sources and warehouses.

Are your data and your policies in agreement?

This question is harder to answer in objective terms than the previous ones. To some extent, it is a judgment call to determine how well policies and data are aligned. To help quantify this there are a few points to consider. First, determine what the organization's goals are and what data is needed to support them. Organizational goals will drive data management goals. If those are clearly defined, the organization probably has a good idea of what questions are being asked and what data is needed to answer them.

Another consideration is looking at what data issues the organization has. Good data governance should give the organization good data, but in the real world, this takes work and leadership. Chronic data issues can take various forms, lack of policy, poorly defined policy, or lack of buy-in to a policy. Either way, the policies need to be examined to determine how to align the data with the policies and procedures.

Finally, data policies need to adapt to changes within and outside of the organization. As the organization evolves, are the data policies examined regularly to ensure they are still in line with the new direction? Are there mechanisms in place to make sure the data keeps up? One high-profile example of this is the recent implementation of data privacy laws in the European Union (EU). Even though no laws changed in the United States, many businesses and organizations with international customers and members determined that they needed to adapt to EU policies and procedures. In a healthy data governance culture, mechanisms would be in place to review how data is collected, stored, and used to ensure it adapts to the new environment.

CHAPTER 3

The Five Buckets of Effective Data Governance

The task of creating effective data governance can seem daunting at first, especially for an organization that has been working for a long time without it. Fortunately, like many large challenges, data governance can be broken down into smaller, more manageable components.

The DAMA DMBOK2 identifies over twenty different "buckets" of data governance, each covering a set of related principles and practices. In this book, we'll cover the five that we consider most important: Data Quality, Data Ecology, Data Privacy and Security, Data Policies, Standards, Processes, and Procedures, and Data Handling. Each focus on a specific aspect of an organization's relationship with its data.

> ### The Core of Data Governance
> *Data Governance* is the strategic activity of maintaining organizational data assets, setting priorities, establishing policies, and reviewing procedures. This work is mostly done at the executive level of the organization with an executive liaison communicating expectations to a mid-level team for execution.

It's important to remember with these buckets that while on the surface they may seem very technically oriented, the business is still an equal partner in data governance. Related to that is a reminder that an organization's business intelligence goals absolutely need to be considered in an organization's data governance.

Even though each of the buckets will be defined and explored separately, none of them is an independent silo. Data governance has the greatest impact when the individual components are well-integrated with each other into a coherent whole.

Data Quality

Data quality ensures sufficiently clean, reliable, and complete data. This may seem like a part of data handling but is more concerned with making sure that all the organization's data sources and systems agree with each other on what things mean and how they should be structured. Data quality ensures trustworthy data that helps the organization meet its larger strategic goals.

Another key feature of data quality is ensuring it maintains its integrity and timeliness as it moves through data systems. This is where things like disaster recovery plans, cleanup, refresh, and archival strategies have value.

Data Ecology

Data ecology is the broad understanding and communication of how the systems that collect, store, and transmit data are structured within the organization. Data ecology helps identify the best tools for the job, based on the organization's data goals. It also keeps track of the interrelationships between the data tools.

While data ecology is very heavily involved in the technology the organization uses, business involvement is key here in making sure that the tech effectively supports the business goals.

Another aspect of data ecology where IT and business need a close partnership is in documenting data artifacts, such as inventories, dictionaries, and glossaries. While IT can define what the data is, the business knows what it means, and it is vital that there is a mutual understanding between the two.

Data Privacy & Security

Data privacy and security has become a very hot issue in recent years. Not too long ago, industry and organizations both thought of data privacy and security primarily in terms of protecting data from criminals. Electronic data such as credit card or bank account numbers, passwords, and personal information have all been exploited by bad actors to commit fraud and identity theft. Nobody who handles data wants to feel responsible for a breach where their members or customers were harmed. An organization identified as the source of a leak or exposure of information can suffer irreparable harm to their reputation or bottom line.

More recently, as the general public becomes increasingly aware of just how much data is being collected, analyzed, and used, people are becoming more protective of their personal information as well. Individuals are expecting more transparency in how their personal data is handled, and there are several countries that have passed or are considering broad based privacy regulations.

To complicate matters, an organization's data ecosphere is very complex. Multiple systems collect and handle data, some of which are provided by third-party vendors, use the cloud for storage and processing, and increasingly include systems outside of a traditional IT-controlled infrastructure such as social media or payment apps. This has made the work of protecting data more difficult, and it is not likely to get any easier in the future.

Data Policies, Standards, Processes, and Procedures

Good data governance relies on a strong data culture, but it also needs to put that culture into practice. Having a comprehensive set of standards, policies, and procedures helps ensure that data governance is consistent in all areas of the organization.

One of the key principles of data governance is that data cannot be siloed within an organization anymore. The only way to take advantage of the sophisticated analysis, insights, and forecasts that modern business intelligence is capable of is for data to be freely shared across an organization. That requires the data to meet high standards for consistency and quality, which need to be reinforced in the broader organizational culture.

Having a comprehensive set of standards, policies, and procedures helps ensure that data governance is consistent in all areas of the organization.

This consistency is fundamental to breaking down silos so that data can be freely shared.

IT has historically hoarded a lot of data. It is only when data are shared freely throughout the organization that the power of analysis, insights, and forecasts of modern business intelligence can be fully harnessed. Consistent standards, policies, and procedures bring clarity and trust to your data operations and form a critical foundation for BI.

Data Handling

Data Handling is the joint effort among IT and business stakeholders to identify, develop, and coordinate procedures and policies that enhance the value of organizational data assets and use. This can encompass all the following buckets. It is about the execution of the decisions that are made in the governance and management areas and is performed by core individuals who have the talents and skills to work these processes.

The ultimate goal is to develop rhythms and routines around working with data so that data governance becomes second nature to the employees instead of feeling like something that is imposed upon the organization's employees. Reinforcing the value of quality data also helps employees see good data handling as a vital part of their work.

Data handling is about managing the data to the metrics of data quality, at all steps of the process, not just at intake. It is a first line of defense against bad data entering or residing with the organization's data ecology.

Beyond the Buckets of Data Governance

Each of these buckets looks at one particular aspect of data governance. As organizations review their existing data governance, they may find they are strong in some and weaker in others. Strengthening all five will go a long way towards building good data governance, but there is one final aspect that makes it all work—data culture. To practice good data governance, the organization must also foster a culture where everybody understands, values, and respects data. While looking at the five buckets, keep the importance of data culture in mind.

CHAPTER 4
Data Quality

"We just don't trust the reports," is something we hear a lot when working with organizations on building good data management and governance. The complaint is often justified, because the business intelligence isn't proving itself reliable or valuable to the people that depend on it.

The current data-driven leadership environment means that executives and managers have access to powerful and comprehensive business intelligence, and they are expected to use it to inform and justify their decision making. So, what happens when the business intelligence fails? The decision makers will hold up the dashboards and reports and forecasts to show that they used the data to the best of their abilities, but the data let them down. Over time, the trust in the intelligence breaks down. The processes of business intelligence keep on dutifully turning data into dashboards, but the organization doesn't rely on them. The investment in the tools and talent becomes a sunk cost producing little value in return.

The failure of business intelligence to tell complete and accurate data stories is frequently rooted in issues of data quality. When the data is incomplete, inaccurate, or no longer timely, it can have a domino effect on many downstream business functions. When data in the system is accurate and reliable, though, it is considered source strong, and can be used for high-quality business intelligence. If the accuracy and/or reliability are low, the data is source weak and can lead to lower-quality intelligence. In an environment where business intelligence at higher levels isn't trusted, business units tend to rely only on data they collect and process themselves. They are less willing to either take in information from outside of their silo or share what they do have. Places where joint decisions need to be made are hampered by a lack of business intelligence targeted at supporting the group effort.

Where quality data really empowers the organization is in helping different business units work together more closely and more efficiently. This is why data quality is the first data governance bucket we're going to look at. Data quality sets the target for the rest of the governance effort. Everything else that follows is put in place to meet the quality standard.

Improving Data Quality

Every organization needs to define data quality on its own, as the definition is unique to each organization. The business intelligence needs, the volume and variety of data available, reliability of sources, and many other factors all need to be considered. The organization's industry may already have established standards of data quality. In addition, the definition of data quality will likely vary depending on the specific type of data being considered.

Once this determination has been made, the organization has a good basis to start building its quality controls. Until the business determines the quality standards, IT doesn't have firm targets in place when configuring systems and writing code.

Where the data itself is concerned, quality control starts at the point of capture. If the data coming into the system is inaccurate and incomplete, it will inevitably affect the quality of everything that comes after. Good data governance considers all the places where data enters the ecosphere. These can be familiar entry points, such as Customer Relationship Management (CRM) systems that are already managed by the organization's IT to ensure data is consistent and compatible with other systems. The business may also be partnered up with IT to be sure that procedures are in place and employees are trained to ensure they are entering accurate information into the systems without introducing errors.

Data enters the system in other ways that may not be obvious, though. Many of these entry points may still be managed by IT, but without an understanding of how they fit into the larger data ecology. With increasing use of business tools that collect and feed data into the system, there are often inputs that IT doesn't own.

Data quality strategies need to account for all these different places where data enters the system. Each point of entry—regardless of who owns it or how much data it introduces—needs to be examined to determine how the data can come in as intentionally and accurately as possible. This can include measures to filter irrelevant data out of the stream, minimize human errors, and ensure the data is compatible with other downstream systems.

What is coming into your ecosphere?

One downside of the massive amounts of data that are being generated and collected is that not all of it is useful or even real. Organizations need to develop methods to prevent low-quality or even malicious data from being collected. If a customer-facing system asks for an email address to get past a certain point, a person may have a throwaway they use for such purposes. This kind of contact may not be useful for a lot of customer data trending. Bad actors may also create multiple dummy accounts with the intention of degrading or skewing an organization's data.

A second consideration at the point of entry is understanding the threshold for reliability. Depending on the business use of the data, the required degree of accuracy can vary. For critical business decisions, where acting off of inaccurate data can have serious consequences on both the organization and its members, the threshold for accuracy is going to be very high. The organization needs to consider the reliability of the source and whether it can even provide accurate enough data for the purpose, or if the data needs to come from somewhere else.

Closely tied to that are the processes and procedures for handling the data to ensure accuracy as it enters different ecosystems within the organization, such as marketing, membership, events, and publication systems. The higher the standard of accuracy, the more system resources and human effort may be required to ensure it is not affected by the collection process. While it would be great if all data in an ecosphere could be verified to be 100% accurate at all times, realistically the effort required to do that would make data collection impossibly expensive and difficult. In addition, depending on the business needs of the organization and the organization's broader contexts, 100% accuracy could provide few additional advantages, making such a goal unnecessary.

Once data is inside the ecosphere, it moves between systems and is often transformed by different data handling processes. Some of these transformations are necessary to allow multiple systems to use the same data. If two systems differ on how they handle a hyphenated last name or the number of characters they allow for an address field, the data needs to be edited to be usable by both systems. Other quality checks make sure that duplicate records aren't being created in error. A billing system may have a record for *Steven S Smith* because that's how their name is written on their credit card, but they use *Steve Smith* as their name when signing up for events on the organization's website. The two systems need a way to identify that they are both dealing with the same person.

Quality control as data moves around the ecosphere is dependent on IT being aware of and facilitating the communication between different systems. If business units are acquiring systems that collect or process data without IT coordination, the kinds of reconciliations and transformations mentioned above cannot be done, leading to lower-quality data.

The third major component of data quality is reconciliation and retention. These make sure that stored data is both accurate and timely.

Reconciliation is like the checks made as data enters the system but is more focused on making sure the data retains its accuracy over time. It is an intentional process to validate that information that has been in the ecosphere for some time is still correct and high-quality. If a customer is prompted to verify their address whenever they log into the system, this is a method of data reconciliation. A monthly batch process that compares the address data in the CRM with the US Postal Service's address verification service is another type of reconciliation. Even though one of these processes asks the customer directly for an update when they interact with the organization, and the other is a periodic automated exchange of data, both processes ensure the best possible address data is in the system.

Retention is important because not all data is going to have the same shelf life. With good data governance and business intelligence goals, data can be evaluated to determine how long it is useful. When looking at how long it takes to keep different data elements, one basic principle is to consider how often the data changes compared with how frequently the organization has the opportunity to update it. If some piece of customer data is likely to change a few times per year, but the organization typically only gets an update when membership is renewed annually, that data may be considered source weak for business intelligence purposes if it was collected more than three months prior. Meanwhile, if there is some other data element that changes very rarely, and the organization has quarterly contact with the customer, that particular data might be considered source strong even if it is several years old.

The other consideration for retention is the threshold of reliability for different kinds of decisions. Just as accuracy requirements are considered at the point of entry, they are also a factor in determining how long data should be retained. Generally speaking, the more critical the business intelligence generated from data, the more current that data supporting it needs to be. A customer's membership status is something that needs to be kept current because it affects so many of their interactions with the organization. The history of a member's committee participation is something that is primarily useful for historical information, so its currency is not as critical.

Challenges to Data Quality

Data quality issues are caused by multiple factors, many of which are difficult to control. A data quality study conducted by Experian in 2016 determined that 56% of data quality problems stem from human error. Other common causes include inadequate staffing or budgets, weak data strategy, and poor coordination between departments. These human factors were larger contributors to data quality issues than having outdated or ineffective technology. While there are ways to mitigate human causes of poor data quality, they all require significant investment in selecting and retaining the best talent, clear policies and procedures, and an organizational culture where people recognize the importance of data and their role in protecting it. With good data governance in place, it's easier to target where the shortcomings are and identify workable solutions to correct them.

The human factors are present in both the business and IT. This reinforces the importance of data management and governance being a joint effort between the two. For example, there is a limit to what IT can do about data entry errors if the business unit collecting the data is not invested in its quality. Meanwhile, the business may have developed a clear, concise set of business intelligence needs, but if IT isn't developing the talent to support the technology, those needs can't be met.

Having a strong partnership also increases the capacity of both parties to identify sources of errors and pool their resources to address them. Data that looks normal to IT may look odd to a business user. If both groups are working together through the development of a dashboard or a report, they have better chances of noticing a data quality problem early on and can start collaborating on a solution from the beginning.

Data quality suffers most at the point of entry. This is where the raw information is collected and brought into the ecosphere. This step is prone to inaccuracy if the data source itself is not reliable; human and system errors can also affect the quality.

Vigilance at the point of entry is vital because of the domino effect. If the data coming in has problems, those problems will carry through and can even become larger at every subsequent step of the process.

Even after data has entered the system, there are still points where the quality can be affected. Any time data is transmitted from one system to another or is processed in some way, it can be changed. Some of these changes are necessary if they are part of a data reconciliation or when data is updated as part of the process itself. However, poor integration of systems can create duplicate records and incorrect alteration or deletion of existing records.

Any human interaction with the data introduces the possibility of additional errors. This can include things like requiring employees to manually copy and paste data from one place to another because there isn't an automated integration between the two systems. Data can easily be duplicated or overwritten in these cases.

To maintain the integrity of data, an organization must have a full understanding of the systems and processes involved as well as a clear data strategy. If the systems are not designed to meet the overall business intelligence needs and goals, incoming data may not be complete, or it may not be collected in a way that it can mesh with data from other systems. With an increasing amount of data being collected and handled by business applications that lie outside of IT, it is even more important for organizations to involve both parties as equal partners in maintaining data quality. Third-party applications can provide a lot of data, but how much of it is accurate, reliable, and formatted so the organization can easily incorporate it? One organization we have worked with noticed some of their intelligence had been initially accurate and reliable but had become less useful over time. By examining where the data was coming from, a large amount of it had been loaded into a system that was disconnected from the rest. So at the moment it was added, it was perfectly good. Over time, though, it was never refreshed from the original source or reconciled against data in other systems. It went from being a source of strong data that provided quality business intelligence to source weak data, with a predictable degradation in the quality of reports and forecasts based on it.

Quality Data Leads to Quality Intelligence

There is no doubt that organizations today have access to a greater volume and variety of data than ever before, and that capacity is steadily increasing. That also means that there is no way to look directly at the data itself and get meaningful insights from it. Decision makers can only use that data if it has been processed into comprehensible, actionable business intelligence.

Business intelligence processes are dependent on having ready access to high-quality, complete, and consistent source data to work with. Feeding bad data into the processes is going to result in inaccurate and unreliable reporting. Using weak or incorrect business intelligence to drive decision making can have serious consequences if the organization invests heavily in the wrong things or fails to foresee an important trend.

The full potential of modern business intelligence is achieved when the entire organization is working together; business units freely sharing information and insights with each other and in robust collaboration with IT. When an organization is working this way and the data is high-quality, powerful business intelligence is available for bold data-driven decision making.

On the other hand, if poor-quality data leads to low-quality business intelligence an organization may not ever get to the high collaboration stage. For business units to see the value in sharing data or working together to generate business intelligence, they must know they can trust their partners. When there is bad data in that system, it is very hard to build and maintain that trust. In such circumstances, a lot of business units tend to pull back and only consider data they've gathered themselves as reliable.

In this environment, even if individual business units find ways to independently produce solid business intelligence from limited data, the organization only gets partial data stories. It is only when the entire organization is working together towards shared business intelligence goals and with a universal commitment to data quality that the best results are achieved.

CHAPTER 5
Data Ecology

Good business intelligence comes about when all parts of an organization are collecting and sharing data. This sharing gives the business intelligence tools a higher volume and variety of data to work with, and with multiple systems working together, information can be updated more frequently and checked for timeliness and accuracy.

For this improved body of data to be available for business intelligence purposes, the organization must first understand all of the systems and tools that are collecting and handling data, and how they connect to each other. From there, the next task is to find ways to optimize the different components and how they relate.

Data Ecology is the understanding and communication of data across the organization. Some of the primary components are the different tools used to collect and handle data, system diagrams showing how the tools interconnect, and the data inventories, dictionaries, and glossaries that help make the data itself usable. The data ecology is not static; it must be flexible and adaptable to changes both within and outside of the organization.

In a healthy data culture, an organization has a deep understanding of both its data ecology and business intelligence goals. This helps the organization get the most benefit out of its existing systems and keep pace as the organization's needs continually evolve.

Single Sources of Truth

A *single source of truth* refers to architectural design where each data element has a master copy stored in a single place. All other systems using that data element to refer to the single source of truth instead of storing their own copies. For example, if the single source of truth for member address information is the CRM database, the billing system will refer to the CRM for address information instead of storing their own copy.

Data ecology can be divided into two core areas—the architecture and interoperability—and we explain both terms in this chapter.

Architecture

Architecture refers to both the software that collects, stores, and uses data, as well as the hardware it lives on. The architecture includes not only dedicated data storage and applications, but also other tools that handle data as part of their normal operation. A database with its own primary and backup server banks is an example of the former, while a billing application used to process membership dues or merchandise purchases is the latter.

The architecture contains tools of various sizes and complexity, depending on what they're used for and how much they communicate with other systems. Even a small organization needs to practice enterprise-level thinking in this regard.

Enterprise-level data architecture has several advantages. It allows the organization to identify a set of tools appropriate for different scales to ensure consistency of data and compatibility between them. It also builds efficiency into the system and reduces redundancy and demands on system resources.

> ### What is Enterprise Architecture?
> *Enterprise architecture* is the process by which organizations standardize and organize IT infrastructure to align with business goals. Part of data ecology is thinking about data at an enterprise scale instead of at the levels of departments and divisions all residing within their own data silos.

A well-developed architecture incorporates things like data hubs and archival storage. *Data hubs* are working spaces where different systems exchange information and resolve any conflicts to maintain overall data quality. Data hubs often use an *Integrated Platform As A Service* application (iPaaS) as an intermediary between other systems to make sure data is formatted and referenced in ways that both systems are able to use it.

Archival storage consolidates data collected by different systems into a small number of repositories. Not only does this make it easier to identify and maintain single sources of truth for the data, but it also reduces the storage space that individual systems take up within the architecture.

Good data architecture can also simplify the connections between systems by identifying what needs to be exchanged between them at the level that best meets the business need. Even with a small handful of systems that handle data, there can be a lot of connections. When additional systems are added, the number of connections grows at a greater rate.

It doesn't take long for any map of the architecture to become a confusing mass of boxes and overlapping lines. For anybody trying to do maintenance or upgrades on those systems, or to add or remove one, just understanding which pieces of data are flowing in and out becomes a major undertaking that is prone to errors and omissions.

Building data hubs and archival storage greatly reduces this complexity

Instead of every system potentially having dozens of connections to other systems, each has only two connections: one to and one from the data hub.

Modifying this kind of data ecology is much easier and opens fewer chances for errors. Instead of having to evaluate multiple interactions between a system and the rest of the ecology, most of the work is in determining what information passes between the system and the hub.

Another principle of enterprise architecture is that data systems need to be powerful and flexible enough to match the organization's current and evolving data needs. They also need to be scaled appropriately for those needs, so the organization isn't investing in capacity that they do not need or cannot use.

Interoperability

The second core area in data ecology is the interoperability, or how data moves over and back, between and among systems. For hubs and archival storage to work, they must all agree on what the data is. There are three major components to interoperability:

A data inventory is a complete map of the existing data assets kept by an organization. This identifies what information is collected, where it is collected, and where it is stored.

An enterprise-level data dictionary is a catalog that captures key data used throughout the organization. This catalog has the information that the systems use to categorize and retrieve data often referred to as *reference data* and of most value to data analysts and personnel in IT. It often describes these data with common metadata attributes such as the field's machine name used by the systems, its *human readable* field name, what type of information it is (text, numbers, yes/no, date), the length of the field, and whether or not it is required data. Any system sending data to a hub or archival storage uses the enterprise-level data dictionary to ensure it is formatted in a way that is compatible with the rest of the architecture.

A *data glossary* is a catalog of business terms and their definitions intended to make sure that the entire organization agrees on what individual data elements represent. The business is heavily involved in developing the glossary, as they are the experts in understanding what the data means.

Where does the data live?

There are currently two major types of data storage, *on site* and *in the cloud*. An organization may use one method exclusively, or a hybrid of the two depending on their resources and needs.

On-site storage is where the organization's servers are physically located in their own data center and are intended to exclusively support local operations. These are typically accessible only when in one of the organization's physical locations, or through a secured VPN connection.

Cloud storage is provided by a third-party host and is designed under the principle that the data be accessible from anywhere at any time on any device. Instead of the organization owning and maintaining the servers and the data center, they lease space on the provider's network. In addition to the increased availability and accessibility the cloud provides, this is often less expensive than on-site storage.

When deciding where to store data, IT and the business need to balance out the needs for security and accessibility to come up with the best solution. Because cloud servers are much more accessible by a wide variety of devices, as well as hosting multiple clients, additional security concerns must be addressed.

In addition to the storage type, there are three main types of repositories where the data lives within the architecture: *data warehouses, data marts,* and *data lakes*. Each of them serves a different purpose, depending on how the data is intended to be used.

Data Warehouses are where the most important data is stored, usually over long periods of time. The warehouse is intended to be highly secure and accurate. As such, very little "work" is done with data in the warehouse itself. It is updated only after data has been verified as clean and accurate by other systems. Because of the high volume of data and the need for additional access security, data warehouses are typically maintained in on-site storage.

Data Marts are places where data is accessed by the operational data hub that supports business operations and data warehouses. A data mart will pull selected data from a data warehouse as a "working copy" where information can continuously flow through it and be updated without affecting the integrity of the parent data warehouse. Data marts can be on-site but are increasingly moving to the cloud to take advantage of the increased availability and access.

Data Lakes are "parked" data that might be useful but doesn't yet meet a core business need or decision. This data may still be used for operational purposes but is not considered critical or valuable enough to subsequently store in a data warehouse. Like data marts, data lakes can be either on-site, or take advantage of relatively cheap cloud storage.

How It Works

With the basics of how the ecology is structured, let's look at how this actually works to get high-quality data into the system.

The process starts with data collection via a system front end. This can be a member-facing web page or an application that an employee uses to enter information. The first step often involves the system collecting some identifying information then querying the hub to determine if the contact is going to update an existing record or create a new one. This is done by comparing the new information with some system of record. For example, in an interaction with a person their name and address may be compared to the CRM database to determine if a record already exists for them or not.

Once that is determined, the system performs its transaction, and submits the information to the operational data hub. If the determination of whether the data is an update or a new record has not already been made by comparing the information with a single source of truth, that will be done now.

The data hub determines where in archival storage different data elements submitted by the system are stored. Records are created, updated, or deleted in the archival storage as needed. Depending on how the data hub, archival storage, and individual systems are designed, the data may be immediately available or might not be updated until a batch process is run.

For IT, there are four major issues when working with enterprise-level data systems: availability, speed, accuracy, and security. Practical considerations mean that most organizations will need to do some give-and-take between these. Security and accuracy are typically of utmost importance because the data itself needs to be protected and of consistently high-quality.

As a result, IT and the business often need to work together to prioritize speed and availability of data for different purposes. If there is data that needs to be available for a system that works around the clock, or if real-time updates are needed, other systems may need to accept reduced availability or less frequent batch updates.

Common Mistakes in Data Ecology

One very common mistake we've seen working with organizations is the existence of "shadow IT." This has become much more prevalent as business tools have become more readily available and designed in such a way that a high degree of technical expertise isn't required to install, configure, and maintain them. When business units no longer need IT to implement technology, they often end up developing their own formal or informal internal support teams. This shadow IT is often very effective at working with the business tech, but the fact that they are not part of IT creates a lot of issues, some of them potentially very serious. They may be collecting duplicate data to what is in archival storage. Not only could the duplicate data be inaccurate because it isn't being reconciled against the master copies, but the duplicate might actually be more current, and it isn't being sent to the master storage to be available to all of the other systems using it. More serious issues with shadow IT can arise if, for example, they are not following the same data privacy and security practices as the rest of the organization.

Another big mistake many organizations make with their data ecology comes in the form of "quirks, islands, and dirt." When developing data governance, special care should be taken to identify these kinds of data.

Quirks are data that is unique to different entities within the organization, or data that relies on some knowledge or experience within a business unit to use or understand it. The Event Management team may classify their hotel deposits differently than other business units do in their financial reporting. Or there may be an employee in member services who knows one particular member always pays their annual dues three months late every year. These quirks may make the day-to-day operations of the business unit more efficient but can affect the accuracy of reporting or analysis of data.

Islands are systems or data repositories that are disconnected from the organization's main data ecology. Sometimes these islands are systems that are not integrated with each other. This can include the example of applications used by the business that also collect data, such as social media, which aren't connected with the more traditional data systems maintained by IT. Data being collected on these islands is not available to the rest of the organization, and the people using it may not be aware that they have valuable data at all or have the knowledge of how to use it effectively.

Islands can also be data sources that are completely disconnected from any other data, such as a spreadsheet on someone's desktop. Islands represent potential missed opportunities to collect and use data for business intelligence. Islands are not always a bad thing. An organization's HR data, for example, is often kept on an island because it doesn't need to interact with any of the business data.

Dirt is, as the name suggests, unclean data. This is data that is inaccurate or incomplete. When dirt is integrated with other data systems, it can seriously degrade the quality of the business intelligence. Note that this isn't a sign of bad data practices. It may just mean that in the absence of data governance, the data was collected and managed without consideration of how it fits in with the organization's overall data ecology and goals. With effective data governance, individual systems are continuously monitored to ensure they are collecting and storing clean data that will integrate smoothly into the overall ecology.

The Benefits of a Healthy Ecology

Developing an understanding of the overall data ecology goes a long way towards helping an organization understand what data it has to work with. That alone is critical to determining what kinds of business intelligence can be produced and helps find data gaps that need to be filled to meet business intelligence goals.

When are the data available?

How often data is refreshed and reconciled varies based on several factors, such as how often it is accessed, how critical the data is for routine operations, and the system resources used in updating it. Some systems are designed to update in real time or near-real time (delays of just a few seconds between data being submitted and updates being available to other users or systems). Others may only update in daily or weekly batch processes. A system that mails monthly newsletters out to members may only need weekly updates, whereas a system storing credit card information for purchases may function in real time.

When the data ecology is configured to align with business intelligence and data governance goals, it will be more efficient, and all the tools will have ready access to the data they need. This is especially true when the ecology is structured around enterprise-level thinking. When centralized archival storage is used, there is a single master copy of any piece of data that is available to the tools. This means that all business intelligence works from the exact same information. There is less duplication of information and a lot more opportunities to keep the data up to date and verify its accuracy. Business intelligence built off high-quality data is more accurate, insightful, and reliable.

CHAPTER 6
Data Privacy and Security

Powerful business intelligence comes from having a high volume and variety of data available. Giving the tools more information increases both the accuracy of the intelligence and the types of insights that are available. This has led organizations to make significant increases in their data collection and use, in an effort to continue getting more value out of their investments in data.

Some of these avenues lie outside of the old model where data collection and handling resided almost exclusively within the IT area. With the bulk of the effort to gather and store the data residing within the technical realm, data security and privacy were more straightforward. Even the business intelligence tools were primarily owned by IT, who would work with the business to determine how the data should be processed.

One common factor in modern data governance is the understanding that good business intelligence comes from a strong, enterprise-wide data culture, one where the entire organization is an active partner in collecting and handling data.

The result of these changes is that IT is no longer the primary guardian of data. This is now a shared responsibility between the technical and business sides of the house. Technical owns the systems where the data lives; however, the business side must own the data.

This decentralization of both the collection and safeguarding of data means good governance is extremely important. Building on the understanding of what data management, ecospheres, and guidance are, the next concern for governance is how those buckets help protect the data.

An organization that doesn't attend to these matters may suffer a failure of data privacy and security that has severe consequences. First and foremost, it damages the trust between the organization and its members and customers. Once that trust is lost it takes a lot of work to earn it back. If the failure is large enough, the organization could find itself in the news, and the resulting bad press could haunt it for years. Depending on what caused the failure, the organization could be held liable for financial damages to members or subject to fines and censure by regulating agencies.

The Differences Between Data Privacy and Data Security

Data privacy and security are often used interchangeably but are two very different things. One refers to the principle that people should have control over their own personal information; the other is the mechanism by which data is protected. An organization needs data security to protect data privacy, but each of these concerns is larger than just where the two interact.

Data privacy refers to two main concerns. One is the ability of individuals to determine how their personal data is collected and used. There are ethical guidelines around data privacy, and a growing body of standards, regulations, and laws governing it. The other is the privacy of the organization's proprietary data and secrets. Both personal and proprietary data are types of information that the organization needs to safeguard.

Data security, on the other hand, is defined as "the processes and associated tools that protect sensitive information assets, either in transit or at rest."[5] An organization needs to have strong, flexible data security to protect all of its data—private, sensitive, or otherwise. Even data that is freely shared outside of the organization needs to be safeguarded to ensure it is not accidentally or maliciously deleted or altered. Some common methods of data security include access control, encryption, masking, erasure, and resilience.

Data Privacy

Data privacy is definitely a very hot button issue these days. As the capacity for collecting and using data increases, the concerns around privacy are becoming larger and more complex. Data privacy isn't only about making sure the data is protected from accidental exposure or intentional misuse. It's also about how the data is used. There are undeniable benefits to using business intelligence to develop effective targeted marketing. Streaming services use vast amounts of customer data to offer up movies and TV shows they think their customers want to see, instead of making them search through thousands of available offerings.

The flip side of the coin is that the public is not always comfortable with the sense that their internet behavior and purchase patterns are being constantly monitored and shared out. Social media companies have been called to testify before Congress over how they use business intelligence

---

5. Gartner Glossary, https://www.gartner.com/en/marketing/glossary/data-security

to determine what content their users see, with accusations that bad actors have tried to use this ability to manipulate the political process.

Good data privacy is built upon both ethical handling of the data and compliance with regulations, standards, and laws—these will drive an organization's overall policies. At the practical level, standards, processes, and procedures that govern how sensitive personal data is collected, processed, and stored need to be developed.

Ethical collection of data comes down to respecting respondents, whether they be customers, members, or other individuals that the organization works with or serves. It may involve resisting the temptation to collect data just for the sake of having it because it's available. The goals for business intelligence need to be created with a mind towards data privacy, and from there, the organization should collect only the personal data needed to meet those goals.

Much like collection, processing of data should be limited to only what meets the existing analysis and reporting requirements and should be done in a timely manner. Business intelligence that asks for data to be collected and held for long periods of time before it is used should be reevaluated to ensure that the organization is balancing the value of the intelligence against respect for data privacy.

Finally, we must be intentional about where we store information and for how long. Keeping sensitive data in a location where it can be accessed by systems or personnel with no justifiable business need can easily lead to data breaches, or worse, to criminal or unethical exploitation. In addition to setting a "shelf life" for data, good governance includes processes and procedures to remove the data. Simply deleting it from a database does not destroy the data itself, and there are a lot of data recovery tools that a bad actor can use to reconstruct it afterwards.

In addition to the ethical responsibilities, organizations have around data privacy, there are a number of standards, regulations, and laws that need to be considered. Many jurisdictions have codified definitions of Personally Identifiable Information (PII) and Personal Health Information (PHI) and have laws on how this information must be handled. One such body of legislation that many people are familiar with is the Health Insurance Portability and Accountability Act (HIPAA), which includes significant provisions for the protection of PHI and restrictions on how it may be used.

The European Union has passed the EU General Data Protection Regulation, a sweeping body of legislation that covers data protection and privacy within the European Union. Even organizations that do not operate within the EU need to be aware of the GDPR, as it has some provisions that cover transactions with or monitoring of people inside the European Economic Area. Japan and Brazil are working on similar laws to protect their citizens. The California Consumer Privacy Act is an example of consumer privacy legislation on a smaller scale, but it is still important for organizations to be aware of and determine if they need to incorporate it into their data privacy governance.

> ### The Brussels and California Effects
> Because the European Union and the state of California are such large markets, their laws often end up influencing the laws and regulations in other political entities, as well as industry standards and practices outside of their immediate borders. Both the EU and California are also known for developing very stringent and comprehensive laws, so meeting their requirements will likely meet or exceed requirements anywhere else. For example, because California's vehicle emission standards are so high, auto manufacturers find it most efficient to have all vehicles they sell in the United States comply with them instead of developing different models for sale in different regions of the country.

Another data privacy consideration comes from industry and professional associations. For example, the Payment Card Data Industry Security Standard is a widely accepted set of guidelines intended to protect people when making credit, debit, and cash card transactions. These may be required for ongoing membership within the larger association. In cases where they are optional guidance, they are still valuable to an organization in developing its own data privacy and security governance because they do represent a set of tested standards and a support network to implement and troubleshoot them.

A lot of organizations are recognizing the need for executive-level leadership where data privacy is concerned. Some have created a Chief Privacy Officer role in their executive leadership. Other organizations are adding privacy as an additional responsibility for another executive. In many cases, the responsibility for privacy is assigned to IT, but it may be better taken up by the chief operations or legal officer.

Data Security

Data security is the mechanism by which data is kept safe. While protecting data privacy is a large part of data security, there is a lot more involved. Sensitive personal data isn't the only data in the ecosphere that needs to be protected. An organization may have non-personal data that needs to be protected from exploitation or accidental exposure. Even data that is not considered sensitive needs to be secured against loss or alteration, such as may happen with a ransomware attack.

Data security uses a number of different tools. Some of the primary ones are access control, encryption, masking, erasure, and resilience.

Access control is a cornerstone of data security. To make sure the data is both protected and accessible, methods need to be in place to determine what systems and staff can access it and under what circumstances. There are several methods to accomplish this. The ones that most readily spring to mind are the technological solutions—password protection, system firewalls, VPNs, and so on. There is also a significant human factor to access control. The people using the tools are often exploited to gain system access. Any successful data privacy and security plan must include training, educating, and socializing staff on their responsibilities in protecting the organization's data.

Sharing Data

There are times when secure data needs to be shared with another trusted entity. For example, a third-party vendor that works with data may need to send and receive sensitive customer information. In these cases, the organization needs to develop data policies, standards, processes, and procedures to define allowable methods of sharing this information. This guidance should account for how sensitive the information is, and what protections are available. For example, an organization may determine that some data may be emailed in the form of an encrypted file with the password sent separately. Meanwhile, other types of information may require a more secure transfer method.

Encryption and masking are like each other. They are intended to make the data unreadable by any system or entity that doesn't have the necessary keys. Both methods can use a lot of system resources, so are typically reserved for high value or especially sensitive data. Data that resides within secure storage may be further encrypted so that even if the database itself is breached, the content is still protected. Another way in which encryption and masking is used is when data is transmitted out of a secure location or system.

Erasure, as a data security method, is like its use in data privacy. Different types of data need to be evaluated to identify how long they should be kept and what measures should be taken to make the data inaccessible and unusable after it has expired.

Resilience means that the data can be recovered if it is ever deleted, stolen, altered, or otherwise rendered unusable. Many people think of resilience primarily in terms of the vulnerability of systems to malware and ransomware attacks, where malicious code gets into the ecosphere and destroys or encrypts data.

However, there are also physical threats to data security as well. Any physical object that handles data—from a server bank in a large data center, down to a thumb drive—is vulnerable to being damaged, destroyed, stolen, or lost. Any of these occurrences may require data to be recovered from a secure and recent backup.

Data Classification

One of the biggest challenges in data privacy and security is determining the appropriate level of protection for any particular element. Developing a classification scheme at the enterprise level can streamline the process. Building a small number of classifications for both the data and the people that can access it makes it easier for different business units and systems to protect it as it is collected and transmitted through the system. A classification system may define data as being either public, sensitive, or restricted, based on how it is used and the potential consequences of it being leaked, lost, or corrupted. Each level of classification may also define a set of users that should have access to create, edit, or view the affected data. For example, the most highly classified data may only be viewable by executive leadership, or senior management and data analysts within the department that collected the data.

Using this approach, data can easily be placed into set containers that already have the needs for security and access balanced out, instead of having to look at each data collection activity and develop rules for its handling individually. Since these classifications are set at the enterprise level, the process of ensuring the security of the data as it is transmitted between business units is also simplified.

Human Factors in Data Security

Over time, hackers have become increasingly sophisticated in using an organization's own employees to access data, in conjunction with or in lieu of malicious software. Already, more than half of all cybersecurity incidents are caused by lack of talent or human failure.[6]

> ## Best of Intentions
>
> The Gartner report referenced a survey from May and June 2022 where 69% of respondents report that they bypassed their organization's cybersecurity guidance in the past 12 months, and 74% said they would be willing to bypass cybersecurity guidance if it helped them or their team achieve a business objective. This is symptomatic of weak data culture, where employees do not consider themselves custodians of the data, but rather see the data as a means to an end.

More organizations are becoming aware of the importance of their "human firewalls" and have started training their employees to recognize and report threats. Despite this, many organizations are still neglecting this training, aren't doing it frequently enough, or are failing to keep it current.

Employees are no longer being targeted by just clumsy phishing[7] emails that even untrained users can identify as being illegitimate. Phishing attempts are getting exceptionally good at spoofing legitimate communication and instilling a sense of urgency to act. Another recent development is called *smishing*, the practice of using text messages claiming to be from colleagues or associates to get information and access.

Artificial intelligence (AI) is definitely an emerging risk for data security where human factors are concerned. Companies have already been using AI for quite some time to interact with customers, like on the chat applets of websites. Artificial Intelligence developers have been using such applications to amass huge amounts of data on how people talk and interact to train subsequent generations of their tools. AI chat tools are now disrupting education because students are using them to write essays and term papers.

As AI improves at mimicking genuine human discourse, it may not take long for chatbots or similar tools to be used to launch convincing social engineering

---

6. SANS Security Awareness, https://www.sans.org/security-awareness-training
7. Term: *Phishing*. Refers to the use of deceptive emails, websites, text messages, and other electronic communication to get employees to give up personal or organizational information or allow direct access to organizational systems.

attacks at several people in an organization simultaneously. Today's data security leaders need to start preparing for that.

These challenges are only going to become bigger over time. Not only are the number of attacks against the people that protect the data getting more frequent and sophisticated, but there is also a tremendous turnover of security experts happening. Gartner predicts that by 2025, 50% of cybersecurity leaders are expected to leave their jobs. Some are retiring, but many are citing workplace stressors as the reason.[8] A strong data culture where leaders feel valued and supported—as well as effective data policies, standards, processes, and procedures—can help an organization retain top talent and keep continuity of its privacy and security operations if there is staff turnover.

Principles of Good Data Privacy and Security

Data privacy and security need to balance several competing demands. Data needs to be both accessible and secure, and data collection needs to be limited but also varied. When developing data privacy and security governance, the organization needs to consider all of these to find the best path forward. Four of the biggest factors affecting this balance are stakeholder concerns, external regulation, business access needs, and business concerns.

Stakeholder concerns are what different parties need from the privacy and security governance. The stakeholders define the information they need and determine how critical it is for that information to be accessible and protected. Each stakeholder is an expert in the data collected and handled in their area, but they still need to work together to ensure the right level of privacy and security is in place. A conflict may arise between event management, which wants a lot of customer data to develop targeted marketing, and member services, which speaks with the customers every day and knows how important their privacy is to them.

External regulations represent standards that the organization needs to comply with or face potential consequences. If the organization does not govern their data up to those standards, civil penalties may result, accreditation may be revoked, or their membership in professional and trade associations may be denied. The challenge with external regulations comes in finding ways that the organization can comply while still remaining true

---

[8] Gartner Predicts Nearly Half of Cybersecurity Leaders Will Change Jobs by 2025, https://www.gartner.com/en/newsroom/press-releases/2023-02-22-gartner-predicts-nearly-half-of-cybersecurity-leaders-will-change-jobs-by-2025

to their own internal mission and goals. External regulations may also be very broad or vague, requiring the organization to interpret exactly how best to put them into practice.

Necessary business access needs are where the business intelligence goals are weighed against the privacy and security needs around the data. If the privacy and security are too generous, the organization risks a leak or breach of the data. If the governance is too restrictive, it is difficult to use the data for timely and robust business intelligence. As mentioned already, overly restrictive privacy and security may also lead employees to create vulnerabilities by continually working around the access policies or controls.

Legitimate business concerns are needs for privacy and security that are not driven by external regulation. The business may determine that certain types of data represent trade secrets, research or intellectual property, relationships with other business partners, and so on. Exposure of this data would not necessarily result in civil litigation or bad press, but could still have negative impacts. For example, data related to an organization's five-year growth plan for a new geographical area could be used by competitors to undercut their efforts.

Safe and Protected Business Intelligence

Business intelligence cannot be separated from data privacy and security. Since the intelligence is built upon data, an organization needs to make sure it has structures in place to keep the data ecosphere safe.

Even though business intelligence is essentially data that has been aggregated and processed, privacy must still be considered when determining how accessible the intelligence is and what means are undertaken to secure it. Even if steps are taken to protect the privacy of the individuals whose data makes up the reports or forecasts, there are still social and ethical concerns about how that data is used. An organization's business intelligence could even be misrepresented by others that get ahold of it. Accidental release or theft of business intelligence built on sensitive information leaves the organization open to civil action, lawsuits, or damage to its reputation.

Since data privacy is concerned with the privacy of the organization in addition to its customers and members, trade secrets, proprietary research, or long-term plans could all be part of or inferred from business intelligence.

Data security also refers to protecting data not only from other entities that should not have it, but also from unauthorized deletion or alteration. A breach of data security allows ransomware access to some or all of an organization's data, which can suddenly become inaccessible. Even worse, if the data is corrupted without the organization knowing, any business intelligence created from it could be disastrously inaccurate. Ensuring the integrity of the organization's data also ensures the integrity of the business intelligence.

CHAPTER 7
Data Policies, Standards, Processes, and Procedures

For business intelligence to be useful, the underlying data needs to be handled consistently. As organizations move towards enterprise-level thinking with their data, the need for consistency over time becomes clear. This is where data policies, standards, processes, and procedures come into play. The first step is to identify the organization's overall business intelligence strategy, and then break it down into tactical goals. With the knowledge in hand of what the data needs to support, the framework around its collection and flow can be built.

Much like the business intelligence needs are considered from the top down, data governance should be as well. Begin with the high-level, long-term strategic goals—data policies and standards, and work towards more granular and adaptive practices in the form of processes and procedures.

Data policies, standards, processes, and procedures should be housed in a single repository where all the guidance is maintained. This allows the entire organization to have ready access to this valuable guidance.

Data Governance Policies

Data Governance Policies guide the executive team in decision making. Essentially, these are the principles and rationale for what the organization is doing and why. Policies apply across the enterprise and should not change frequently.

When developing policies, it is important to remember that they do not address how something should be done, only the what and why. Policies are related to the long-term vision of the organization. They are not intended to react to shorter-term goals, changes within and outside of the organization, or emerging technologies. Rather, they give the organization stability and a sense of direction to allow it to adapt to changes.

Data Standards

Data standards are a body of reference points that describe how data is collected and recorded. These can come from within the organization, or from external sources.

Internal Data standards are jointly created by the business and IT, to make sure that the data is handled appropriately. External sources of data standards include government regulation and industry best practices. Two examples of external sources of data standards are the General Data Protection Regulation, which is legislation passed by the European Union to protect the data privacy of its citizens and the Payment Card Industry Data Security Standards, developed to assist organizations in protecting customer and member account data.

Both internal and external standards need to be reviewed regularly to ensure they remain current and reflect the environment the organization is working in. With external standards it is especially important for the organization to continuously monitor trade publications and upcoming legislation to be aware of upcoming changes. Ideally, an organization should start identifying necessary updates of their own internal standards, processes, and procedures before a new law is passed or external standard published.

Another concern for organizations is reconciling different standards with each other. The state of California recognizes a wider range of racial demographic categories than the federal government does. If an organization works with state agencies, it may need to change its standards around this data.

In many cases, organizations must balance out different needs when it comes to their data, and having good standards helps. To have good business intelligence data needs to be available to the tools, but some types of data need to be protected or kept confidential. Having organizational standards around these kinds of sensitive data ensures that it is stored and transmitted appropriately. Other standards may identify how long different types of data are valid, what is needed to consider data reliable, and what types of metadata are needed.

Data Processes

Processes lay out the general actions to be taken regarding the collection and transmission of data. An area's data processes should cover most cases where data is handled, and they are where the policies and standards are really put into action.

Unlike policies and standards, which are created at a high level and intended to apply across the organization, processes may be specific to divisions, departments, or other business units. Processes will also change more frequently, to keep up with the organization's operations.

Data Procedures

Procedures spell out the specific actions employees take to initiate, maintain, and sustain a policy and adhere to the process and standards. The procedures make sure that the day-to-day operations of the organization are collecting and handling the data properly, that it is complete, accurate, and protected.

Plotting Your Course

Even though the body of data policies, standards, processes, and procedures is not a single stand-alone body of work, it still does follow an orderly hierarchy. In effective data governance every procedure or practice that involves data is part of a larger process. Each process then points back to specific standards, and ultimately up to enterprise-level policies.

Since data is often collected and handled as parts of other operations, most of an organization's data procedures are not stand-alone documents. They are often incorporated into other procedures. Effective data governance and culture ensures that as procedures for other tasks are developed, places where data is handled are identified and reviewed to ensure compliance with processes and standards.

From Policy to Procedure

The structure of policies, standards, processes, and procedures is not strictly hierarchical. The policies and standards are situated at the top and define the data governance goals, while the processes and procedures describe how to meet them.

Every procedure that involves data does have to comply with standards and policies. The way this works is that every procedure is part of a process. The processes, in turn, ensure the procedures support the policies and maintain the data standards. The structure of data policies, standards, processes, and procedures can be roughly pyramidal, with a policy guiding several standards. Underneath the standards and policies will be a set of processes and procedures that support them. To note, though, there may still be policies, standards, processes, and procedures that are not 100% correlated with each other or arranged into neat hierarchical structures.

In general, however, a path can be drawn from a policy down to a specific procedure. For example, how would a teacher respond to a request for student information in a way that complies with policies and standards?

One of the organizational policies centers the protection of student privacy. Note that this policy states the commitment, but does not dictate how it will be accomplished.

The data standards have determined that certain types of student data are protected as private information. Because of this classification, there are limits on who within the organization may request the data and for what purposes.

To comply with the student privacy policy and security standards, there is a process in place where any question about a student that isn't from a parent or guardian needs to be referred to the principal. At this level, the what and why of the policy is being transformed into guidance on how it should be done.

Finally, to support that process, there is a procedure for teachers to follow when they receive a request for information. The teacher is required to inform the requestor of the student privacy policy and the procedure for requesting information. The teacher will then ask the relationship between requestor and the student, and why they need the information. This is forwarded to the principal, who is required to respond within one business day, or quicker if necessary.

The Principles of Good Data Policies, Standards, Processes, and Procedures

Good data governance is dependent on having a unified vision of what that looks like. All levels of the organization, from executives to customer service, need to have consistent guidance on how to collect and handle data. The processes and procedures must also fit into the existing workflows so that good data habits become second nature instead of feeling like an added burden.

Looking at that guidance, it needs to balance stability and adaptability. This is why the overall policies are intended to be very broad in outlook and change only rarely. The policies don't need to adapt to new technologies or social trends. Instead, the policies stand firm to give the organization a strong sense of its commitments and values, to make sure that it absorbs those changes in a way that continues to protect its data and make the best use out of it.

Moving down from the policy level, the guidance becomes more specific and more flexible at the same time. As new regulations or technologies emerge, as organizations consider their ethical responsibilities and the threats they face, standards need to keep pace. The same goes for the policies and procedures—these govern the activities where data is actually collected and handled. In a rapidly changing social and technological landscape, these need to be constantly updated.

When an organization has good data governance, the mechanisms are in place to allow the daily procedures to change as needed, while still remaining in compliance with the overarching standards and policies.

Data policies, standards, processes, and procedures are also only as good as the culture that supports them. Dozens of detailed, exacting procedures mean nothing if there's no investment in following them. The best BI tools in the world can't provide quality analysis and forecasting if there isn't a serious commitment to providing the best data to support it.

Common Mistakes

The biggest shortcomings we've observed working with organizations are a lack of policies to anchor data management, a weak data culture, or a lack of overall structure to their policies, standards, processes, and procedures.

Strong policies are the foundation of data policies, standards, processes, and procedures. They help define what the organizational data culture is, and they give the executives and higher levels of management a constant touchstone to use in decision making. If privacy protection is an organizational policy, it becomes an organizational priority. Every change to the data ecosphere is evaluated through a lens of protecting data privacy. Every time a decision maker hears of a new privacy protection tool or threat, they are reminded that the organization takes care of its data. This commitment means that the decision maker considers what the change means for their area of responsibility, and they act if necessary.

The policies are the stable anchors that ensure the procedures can adapt to changes while still contributing to the overall data goals. If there aren't organization-wide data standards, the processes can result in different areas producing conflicting data, which leads to poor business intelligence. When business intelligence is unreliable, business units tend to retreat into silos, where they only trust data that they themselves have collected or processed. In contrast, developing well-structured data policies, standards, processes, and procedures makes sure all data activities are working towards common goals and standards.

A Framework for Better Business Intelligence

When an organization doesn't have structured data policies, standards, processes, and procedures, it can lead to fragmented data or problems with data being shared between systems and business units. When the business and IT work together to develop this body of work, though, it gives the business intelligence tools a more consistent and standardized body of data to work with. This makes the entire business intelligence process not only more accurate, but also more efficient.

Without having strong policies, standards, and processes, an organization can still find itself having a lot of great procedures being written by its individual business units. This can lead to good, but limited, business intelligence that is reliable for that unit's operations, but may not be globally applicable. When a business unit with good procedures shares data with one that is not as strong, the resulting business intelligence is not as good.

The best business intelligence is going to come from a lively and interconnected data ecosphere. The more readily data can be shared across the enterprise, the rawer information is available to the tools to generate accurate reports and forecasts. A higher volume of quality, consistent data leads to higher accuracy and reliability in the reporting. When all the data in the ecosphere has been collected and handled to a consistent standard, each of the business intelligence tools also has a wider variety of data on hand, which can lead to more creative insights and flexibility in forecasting against different scenarios.

CHAPTER 8
Data Handling

Business intelligence initially emerged as computers were developed for military and security services. From there, commercial enterprises started automating their systems. For quite a while, the start-up costs of acquiring the hardware, software, and supporting talent limited it still to larger companies. Once PCs became powerful enough to aggregate spreadsheets into data visualizations, business intelligence started to become accessible to smaller organizations. When Microsoft Excel added things like coding and scripting abilities and charting functions in dropdown menus in the early 1990s, it became a rudimentary business intelligence tool.

Since then, the tools and skills needed to gather data and extract good business intelligence from it have become much more powerful while also becoming more accessible to smaller organizations. The technology has become a lot cheaper, and the talent pool that can support is much wider. So, with all this available, why do organizations still struggle with getting quality business intelligence from their efforts?

In many cases, the shortcoming is in their overall data handling. In previous chapters, we've looked at four other buckets of data governance, and they've all shared one thing in common: the business and IT need to provide oversight of the data itself. Data handling is the process of developing procedures to ensure timely, accurate, and relevant data. This includes removing duplicates and correcting incorrect data as it enters and moves through the data ecosphere.

The benefit to the organization is that as the rhythms of data handling become embedded as routines, the data improves, which strengthens the resulting business intelligence.

Data Handling and the Other Buckets

In a way, data handling is the component of data governance that is closest to the data itself. While the other buckets are strongly associated with defining the data environment or determining what should be done with data and why, data handling focuses a lot on how the organization governs its data.

On the surface, data handling looks a lot like it's part of the data quality bucket. However, quality sets the standards that data must meet, regarding its accuracy, reliability, and timeliness. Data handling is more about having the structures in place that let the organization continuously monitor and improve the quality of its data. Data handling supports the mission of data quality but is still separate from it. For example, a data quality requirement would be that all member records include an email address. Data handling executes this by ensuring that systems capturing member information must include an email address field.

Personally Identifiable Information (PII)

PPI is generally defined as information that can be used to identify a person. There are ethical standards and regulatory requirements related to PPI when working with personal data. We will cover this in more depth in the chapter on data privacy and security but want to emphasize here as well that organizations need to be very attentive to what PPI they have and how they protect it.

The organization cannot separate IT and the business where quality of data is concerned. Without input from the business on the meaning of data, and the importance and criticality of different elements, IT doesn't have the context to make meaningful decisions on what is and is not quality data. Looking at something like the retention of data, without business input IT doesn't have a business justification for deciding how long to maintain different data elements. IT could look at how often a data element changes versus how frequently updates are available to make a best guess, but it's still a guess. Business intelligence built off of data that is managed by guesswork is not going to be reliable. Only the business is able to look at what they do with the data to determine whether some element is valid if it was last updated two years earlier, or if they don't trust it if it's more than six weeks old.

> ## *iPaaS and the Cloud*
>
> iPaaS stands for Integration Platform as a Service. According to Gartner's IT Glossary, iPaaS "is a suite of cloud services enabling development, execution and governance of integration flows connecting any combination of on premises and cloud-based processes, services, applications and data within individual or across multiple organizations." When using cloud storage or cloud-based applications, iPaaS can perform the function of middleware between the organization and its cloud partners..

On the flip side of the coin, the business may want to have a daily reconciliation of several databases with external sources to look for errors or duplicate records. This is a lofty goal, but IT knows what system resources they have available to run reconciliation reports and may have to work with the business to prioritize data that gets a daily reconciliation as opposed to a weekly report run.

As an organization initially maps out their data ecology, and then maintains it over time, data handling is a huge factor. Part of the data ecology is understanding and defining all the systems that collect, communicate, and process data, as well as the connections among them. Data handling is what makes sure that data is not duplicated as it moves between those different systems, or incorrectly altered or deleted.

Successful data ecology is based on enterprise-level thinking about data. It takes it out of the realm of multiple systems establishing ad hoc connections between themselves, and builds a centralized structure with archival storage, and data hubs, warehouses, and lakes. Without a well-defined and structured data ecology, data handling is extremely difficult, as each connection in a complex web of systems must be individually examined and defined. Yet with good data ecology, the data handling effort has to oversee fewer connections, which leaves more time and attention to make the connections cleaner and more efficient.

One of the data handling tools that helps a lot in supporting a healthy data ecology is middleware. This is software or some other automated process that acts as an intermediary between other systems to make sure data is formatted and referenced in ways that both systems can use it. Looking at an earlier example of two different systems that allow different maximum field lengths for an address, there would ideally be a piece of middleware that would edit the address to meet both systems' requirements. While middleware is the tool, data handling is the process where the business and IT look at the two systems' data requirements and decide what the tools and processes should do to the data to make it compatible with both systems, without losing its meaning to the business.

Depending on the size of the organization and the number of interconnected data systems, different types of middleware may be required. API scripting is useful for a small number of systems that are using data elements that don't change much. This type of scripting defines how specific data elements need to change to be usable by specific systems. If one system stores dates as MM/DD/YYYY, and another as YYYY:MM:DD, an API script would reformat dates every time data is transmitted to make sure they are usable at the destination. Relying on API scripts becomes much more difficult as the number of connected systems increases, especially if there are many different data formats in use.

Integration Platform as a Service (IPaaS) is a better option for more complex ecospheres, especially ones that are built on enterprise-level thinking with external storage, data warehouses, and so on. IPaaS does more than just edit data to make it compatible between systems, it also works to get different systems to interact more efficiently and accurately as a whole.

When considering the Data Policies, Standards, Processes, and Procedures, data handling is a large part of this. The policies describe the organization's guiding principles where data is concerned. When developing data handling processes and procedures, they need to comply with and support those policies. The standards set criteria for how the data should be collected and stored. The processes and procedures that follow from the policies and standards are the backbone of the organization's data handling and are needed to develop the routines and rhythms that make data handling second nature to the organization.

Without having a good grasp of the mechanics of data handling, the tools and human factors that go into categorizing and defining data and monitoring its quality, it's hard to put the policies and standards into action. A policy to protect customer or membership data and a standard that members' Private Personal information (PPI) can only be accessed by a specific subset of internal users if they have a legitimate business need is a great start.

The organization still needs processes and procedures to define what data needs to be protected as member PPI. It needs to identify which users may access the information and how they provide business justification. The organization needs the technology that can restrict access to member PPI unless certain criteria are met. This is data handling. Without it, the organization runs the risk of either failing to protect personal privacy, or making protected data so difficult to access that it cannot be used operationally or for business intelligence purposes.

This example also explains the relationship between data handling and data privacy and security. There must be a balance between protecting data and making the data available when it is needed. Data handling lets the organization find that balance point by developing an understanding of data classification and the different ways people can access it. Consistent data handling means that all areas of the organization have compatible methods to identify sensitive data and procedures for collecting, storing, and using it. This reduces the risk of accidental exposure or breach of data when it moves between systems and business units.

When considering data protection, the business needs to understand where protected data is potentially visible and accessible during operations. IT has the tools and expertise to identify protected information and put restrictions around it, but it is the business that determines at which points in their normal procedures the information needs to be hidden or masked, and when it does need to be visible and editable—and by whom.

Case Study

We worked with an organization that replaced their Association Management System (AMS). They hoped to get not only a newer product with more powerful features, but also better membership data. The transition to the new system was smooth as far as day-to-day operations went. But after two years, they were still having significant problems with their data collection and analysis. The poor data quality meant business intelligence was unreliable and gave them little confidence in any analysis or forecasts they were making from it.

Initial interviews with staff showed that their data suffered from duplicate entries, missing data, and incorrect information. In some cases, older data was simply overwritten by newer entries. Not only did this corrupt the current data in the system, but valuable historical data was also lost.

While the new AMS was a very powerful tool, that power came with a cost in the form of very complex data handling structures. There were a lot of inputs and outputs and multiple integrations with other applications. Each of these is a potential entry point for errors. Another issue was that the AMS pushed a lot of data out to other applications, but did not take much in. Good data handling requires applications to have robust two-way communication with each other—outgoing data is compared with incoming data to be sure that both applications agree with each other.

These were the kinds of problems that the organization was having. The different applications were not communicating properly, resulting in one data source after another becoming corrupted. These may have been small errors introduced into the body of data, but when multiple applications were involved, each of which had a small number of errors, the overall effect was a body of data that was unreliable.

We looked at some short-term fixes to address the immediate problem and are continuing to work with them to establish better integration through IPaaS, while also adding tools, processes, and procedures to manage duplicates and perform address validation to ensure timely, accurate, and reliable data.

Common Mistakes in Data Handling

The biggest mistake in data handling is looking at it solely as an IT responsibility. The context has shifted, and now the business must be actively engaged in data handling. While IT has traditionally owned the bulk of an organization's data technology, the business is increasingly using its own tools that collect, communicate, and process data. To protect the quality and integrity of an organization's data, the processes, and procedures around it have to be consistent across the board.

Data handling also suffers when IT doesn't understand the importance and use of different data elements. Some data has higher security requirements than others. Some data has higher accuracy requirements, or a shorter shelf-life. IT doesn't have the in-depth understanding of what the data means to be able to classify it or determine how frequently it should be reconciled, archived, or destroyed. Without the business being actively involved in data handling, the best IT can do is guess at these requirements.

Finally, even when IT manages the tools that collect and use the data, it's often a business process that gets the data into the tool or instructs the tool how to use and analyze the data. Good data handling means that the business understands how the tools work and what they need. When business and IT are collaborating well, customer-facing employees have procedures in place to enter data cleanly, or even spot inconsistent or bad data as they encounter it.

Getting the Best Results

With so many great data and business intelligence tools available to organizations today, a lot of information can be presented to managers and executives. It's easy to pull together an attractive dashboard or several reports that project the outcomes of different decisions. These can present very compelling data stories, but if they are built on inaccurate or incomplete data, they can lead an organization down the wrong path.

As more data comes into the system from an increasing variety of sources and it is transmitted through a complex ecosphere, it needs to be continuously monitored. Part of data quality is timeliness, meaning organizations want to keep bringing in fresh data to be sure it's current. If four or five different systems and applications are collecting customer data, there is a big risk of creating duplicate records or corrupting existing data. It's data handling that gets those systems working together to keep the data quality up.

What data handling does for an organization is provide the tools it needs for proper oversight of the data. The organization understands that business and IT must work together to determine what each element needs, and then work together to create the processes and procedures to clean up duplicate and incorrect data. It is also very important that both IT and the business acquire and grow the talent necessary to support their data handling efforts. Data handling requires not only people with technical skills to handle the software and hardware, but also good business partners that are well-versed in the standards, best practices, and regulations that govern how data comes into, flows through, and is used by an organization.

In some ways, this is where data governance works most closely with the data itself. When an organization invests in data handling it is investing in the integrity of its data. When the data itself is reliable, that makes the business intelligence that comes from it more reliable as well.

CHAPTER 9
Data Culture

Over the past few decades, the number of people involved in the collection and handling of data within an organization has markedly increased. It is no longer the realm of a corner of IT that is designated as a dedicated data team. There are a lot more people both in IT and the business that touch data. Many of them don't realize that they are actively working with valuable data—it's not in their job title or description, and they're not routinely accessing a database or logging into a visualization app. Yet they're providing a lot of the data the organization uses to develop its business intelligence. This begs the question of how reliable can business intelligence be if a good number of people handling the foundational data don't realize how important of a role they're playing?

When employees or business units don't understand how many routine operations can collect or generate useful data for BI, they may not be thinking about how the work they do or the tools they use affect the data ecosphere.

Even those employees that know they are collecting or handling data may not be well-versed in the policies and standards that help ensure its quality. They may not have the training needed to protect it, or even a full understanding of what is and is not data.

Considering that any chain is only as strong as its weakest link, an organization has to be sure that there is good data governance in place throughout its organization. One weak source of data or a system that is not compatible with others can have a ripple effect that can lead to unreliable or inaccurate business intelligence.

This is where organizations need to foster cultures of data stewardship. From the highest levels of leadership down through directors, managers, and supervisors to the employees doing the day-to-day work, everybody needs to understand and value the data in their care. Communicating the value of good data governance is critical to establishing and maintaining data culture.

How do workers relate to their data?

For a lot of people who don't work in a role with explicit data responsibilities, data governance can seem like something that other people do somewhere else. They think about data rarely, if ever, when performing their daily tasks.

A lot of employees may have an ambiguous or even hostile relationship with data if they are only exposed to it in the context of performance evaluation. When the only dashboards a person sees are at team meetings or performance reviews, it can feel like organizational data is a means of reducing them to just numbers and cogs in a machine. When a chart goes up on the wall every quarter and the message every time is that the department needs to increase membership numbers again, it's easy for people to see data as something that's imposed upon them and used as a means of constantly moving a goalpost.

This does not build a healthy data culture. This is not to say that tracking performance metrics as a means of continual, iterative improvement is a bad thing. But to really build a strong data culture, the value of data to the organization as a whole needs to be clear to everybody. The benefits to the organization, and by extension to its employees, have to be communicated.

Building a Sense of Stewardship

When building a data culture, the goal is to make sure that the entire organization understands the importance of data, as well as individual roles in collecting and handling it. If this thinking is not already in place in an organization, a good first step to building culture is to promote stewardship of the data and processes.

For a long time, IT has typically "owned" organizational data and the tools that work with it. This put the responsibility of maintaining its quality with the technical teams. Even within IT, there were often distinct data units that were the custodians of the data, and thus were seen as the experts on collecting and handling it.

The result is a lot of people not feeling any responsibility for data or the processes and procedures around it. Even people that might be directly involved in collecting it seldom feel any particular stewardship over it. They do their jobs, most of them conscientiously and committed to doing them well, but those activities they did that put data into the system are just tasks they do. An organizational event coordinator may not ever consider themselves to be a data collector or even think about how information they gather is used to develop business intelligence.

For a modern, data-driven organization, that old kind of thinking simply does not work anymore. Data is everywhere in an organization and today's business intelligence tools want to pull it all together for analysis, reporting, and forecasting. This requires a culture of data governance from top to bottom, business side and IT together.

At a high level, the executives build data policies that are then used to develop standards. From there, the processes and procedures that address daily operations are written. Part of maintaining a good data culture is making sure that any data activities and their importance to the organization are included.

Let's take, for example, the issue of protecting the privacy of members' personal data. When member service representatives are trained on an update to the CRM, this should include the places where personal information may be visible on a page. Emphasize that this is protected data that criminals target, and that it cannot be given over the phone unless the procedure for verifying the caller's identity has been done.

This gives the representatives a sense of stewardship over the data they see in the CRM and their role in protecting it. Getting the identity verification before releasing information isn't just a thing they do because they've been told to do it; rather, they understand that there is a really good reason for it.

Imparting the importance of data on the people who work with it can also increase the accuracy and reliability of it. Just like emphasizing the importance of protecting private data, really communicating how information is used in decision making helps employees feel invested in the quality of their work as they handle data.

Deepening Joint Stewardship

Fostering a sense of individual stewardship throughout the organization is only the first step, though. A common trap when thinking of stewardship is a sense that every individual has a responsibility for a well-defined and self-contained set of data elements or procedures that they directly contact. It's great for the membership services team to feel individual stewardship over personal protected data and see themselves as a human firewall built around it. But there's a lot more they could be a part of.

Joint stewardship is the next level beyond individual stewardship. Joint stewardship aims to protect the confidentiality, integrity, and availability of data across the organization. It is the process for maximizing the value of data as an organizational resource.

With joint stewardship in place individual users recognize that the data they collect and work with isn't owned solely by themselves. It goes beyond just understanding that data should be moving between different business units, to knowing that accurate data moving freely benefits the entire organization. Going from mere individual stewardship to joint stewardship creates an environment where business units can place more trust in data that they did not collect themselves. It can make them more confident in sharing their data with other units without worrying that it may be lost or incorrectly altered by other users.

Sharing data freely gives different parts of the organization a higher volume and variety of data to use for developing business intelligence. Event management, member services, and billing may all capture different types of customer demographics. When that information flows between them, each business unit has a more holistic view of the organization's customers than any of them alone. This also opens more opportunities to verify and correct customer data, leading to an overall increase in accuracy and timeliness.

Furthermore, joint stewardship also means empowering people to act on data issues. This can take the form of the business identifying improvements and driving projects to update code or systems in IT. It can also mean individuals within the organization stepping up when they see problems and being supported by their leadership.

As an example, we worked with one organization where a serious conflict developed between a senior researcher and a data manager. The data manager had designed some analysis tools to work in a very specific way. A senior researcher with an advanced degree refused to follow those procedures and was getting very different results. The data manager, being the one who worked most closely with the source data and the tools, tried to work with the researcher on the correct procedures. Unfortunately, the researcher waved their more senior position and PhD around, and became increasingly hostile to the manager to the point of bullying them. In our review of this case, we had to have a conversation with the data manager's leadership about how they should have stepped in to back their employee. While the researcher had education and standing within the organization, the data manager was providing good stewardship over the data by developing a workable system that protected its quality and integrity. In a healthy data culture, the data manager would have received the support they had earned and that they needed in the conflict.

To truly support data culture, joint stewardship must be included in job descriptions and performance evaluations for employees who collect and work with data. The expectation that the employee is a caretaker for data must be made clear up front, and regularly reinforced.

Building the Culture

The ultimate foundation of a good data culture that goes past individual stewardship and into joint stewardship is trust. IT and the business need trust between each other and within themselves such that they are working toward the same goals and providing the same level of commitment.

One major component to this, of course, is having consistent and clear data policies, standards, processes, and procedures. The data policies and standards should be applicable to the organization as a whole. IT should not be working under different policies and standards than marketing and billing and member services.

Since the policies and standards then drive the processes and procedures that are specific to individual business units' core departments, there is a good basis to ensure that at an operational level, reliable data is being collected and is maintaining its integrity as it moves around the ecosphere.

For data governance to work, executive leadership must visibly make it a priority. They can't just make directives that the organization will be data-driven and expect excellent business intelligence to fall out of the sky. They need to demonstrate that they trust the data they are given, and that they are using it as a basis for their decisions.

> ## *Commitment*
> At the end of the day, a policy is only as strong as the organization's commitment to following it, and a procedure is only as good as the person who performs it.

This needs to carry on through the org chart, each level working with the ones above and below it to make data stewardship a way of life. Since senior leadership is advising the executive level, they need to determine what intelligence they need to deliver and work with their people to make sure that there is active communication and collaboration happening. They need to make sure that their subordinates are comfortable with the information they're providing and confident that their peers are working to the same level.

The five data governance buckets are dependent on data culture running through the organizational hierarchy. Each level needs to be accountable to the ones above and below it for sending up good intelligence and/or data, and providing guidance, leadership, and support to the levels below.

One thing that is critical to building a data culture is for leaders to understand their people's concerns with the extra requirements and expectations that come with implementing data governance. When a process adds three or four additional data collection or validation steps to every call member services takes, a manager needs to be prepared for the pushback when the supervisor points out they're also being asked to reduce overall call times. The marketing director may ask how they're supposed to add a technical project manager to work with IT on integrating new business apps when there's also a headcount freeze. Being empathetic and understanding and willing to work together shows that data governance is a cultural value for the organization.

When data governance is well-developed within an organization, it will eventually become second nature. The extra work necessary to manage the data effectively should be offset by gains in efficiency and productivity and overall growth of the organization.

There needs to be a culture shift within the organization to get to that point, though. After data governance is well-embedded, the culture must still be maintained to make sure that everybody continues to be good data stewards and that the organization is primed to continue to evolve as the world around it changes.

Can the culture be measured?

There are few good ways to measure how well a concept or a practice has become part of an organization's culture. There isn't a standard unit of adoption or metric of belief that some business intelligence tool can display on a dashboard.

Some indirect measurement can be made. An organization can determine how many of its employees take data privacy and security training in a timely manner and how well they do when IT launches a fake phishing campaign to see if the learning took root. Trending of error rates in data entry over time can be done, or actual growth in different markets can be compared with projected growth to see how well the forecasts performed.

It is still possible to get a feel for whether data culture is fortifying data governance. The challenge a lot of organizations are up against today is that their business intelligence isn't living up to its full potential. Reporting isn't always accurate; the forecasts are not always hitting. Digging deeper, organizations are finding a lot of this comes down to weaknesses in the underlying data, disconnected data sources, incompatibilities between systems, and business units that don't work together.

Fostering a healthy data culture to drive acceptance of data governance within the organization will eventually show its worth. Measure by measure, data quality will improve. Joint efforts and collaboration will be visible and produce more interesting and deeper insights. The business intelligence will become increasingly reliable. People will trust it more and will know how to ask the right questions to make sure the data is actually telling the right data story for their needs. There may not be an objective yardstick to measure data culture, but consistent results will speak for themselves.

CHAPTER 10

Talent Development Within the Organization

Much of the discussion up to now has focused on creating organizational structures and culture to build awareness of how ubiquitous data is within an organization. By making everybody a data caretaker, the goal is to optimize the data going into business intelligence tools.

This does not eliminate the need for the organization to have dedicated data experts and specialists. Rather, the intent is to allow data teams to spend less time troubleshooting problems with the data and more time optimizing it to meet business intelligence needs.

Different roles within the organization perform their data management duties differently. At the executive level, it takes the form of guidance and vision and developing policies. IT cares for data by managing tools and systems that work with it. For public-facing roles, part of being a data caretaker means thinking about data privacy during every call or email with a member.

There is also the concept of an actual data steward, somebody whose work with data gives them the authority to make tactical decisions around it. Because every organization is different, and all the roles within it are different, there is no one-size-fits-all approach to acquiring and developing data literate talent.

The concept of talent development within the organization's data teams isn't limited to the technical staff that work with the systems and applications. Modern data governance is an equal partnership between the business and IT, requiring both to have data experts. The degree to which they understand the nuts and bolts of the data systems and processes varies by where they sit in the organizational hierarchy. Strategic-level planners need to develop policies and standards, which require them to be more in tune with the principles of good data governance. At the tactical and operational levels, more in-depth understanding of tools and processes is needed. These people are working at a very granular level with the data and need to be proficient with the tools and systems that handle data and develop business intelligence.

Even at the senior leadership and executive levels, some roles will require a fuller understanding of data than others. To get the fullest benefit from business intelligence there need to be top-level decision makers that can keep up with the jargon, and that have developed the skills and experience to provide well-informed leadership.

Organizations need to identify where the experts reside. Some of the experts are obvious, because they have a data-centered role or job description such as a data scientist or engineer. Some of the experts are not as clear, because they may play another role within the organization but are still involved with or dependent on data to a degree where they need to have a deeper understanding of it. Not all of the data experts are going to reside in IT, either. For the business to be an effective partner to IT in data governance, they need to bring their own expertise to the table as well.

The size, composition, and staffing needs of the organization will all play a big role in how talent is developed. A large organization may be able to have dedicated data governance and stewardship roles, large standing committees, and teams of people managing different aspects of governance. An organization of twenty or thirty people may need to look at data roles as additional responsibilities, outsourcing these roles, or bringing in consultants as needed for periodic reviews or to support larger efforts to implement or enhance data governance efforts.

Critical Data Knowledge and Skills Areas

When looking at people whose jobs are defined by data work, there are three critical knowledge and skills areas most of them fall into: *data engineers, data scientists,* and *data interpreters*. These are broad categories, not intended to be a comprehensive list of the data-centered job descriptions.

Working closest with the data sources and the different systems and applications that make up the data ecosphere are the *data engineers*. These are IT assets that manage the hardware and software infrastructure that moves, stages, and develops data. Because of the increasing number of tools that introduce data into the system or work with it, data engineers need to be flexible and adaptable in the types of systems and applications they can support. Modern data engineers can no longer be experts in traditional, IT-managed data tools alone. CRM applications, web applications, social media, and many more are now collecting and handling data. At a minimum data engineers need to understand the interactions between these tools and the rest of the ecosphere.

For smaller organizations, there may not be an in-house data engineer role. Depending on the organizational structure and the capabilities of the employees, the IT director or even the CIO takes on the responsibility of ensuring that any systems that collect or handle data work well together. This often takes the form of coordinating with the engineers of the different applications to ensure they are compatible with each other. This requires the responsible person within the organization to have a good understanding of how all the systems and tools fit together.

The next category is the *data scientists* who work with large data sets. Data scientists use specialized tools to process, model, and analyze the data to determine what it means. Because of the sheer volume of the data sets, a lot of the work is done via some form of automation, including machine learning and artificial intelligence. Data scientists use their technology to extract information that meets specific criteria to perform statistical analysis and model different scenarios.

At the opposite end of the information chain from the engineers are the *data interpreters*. These are people with skills and experience in making sense of the data, in both visual and narrative formats. The data interpreters are the ones who look at the questions being asked of the data, and essentially produce the basic business intelligence that is then further refined before delivery to its intended audiences. Good data interpreters are not only technically savvy with the business intelligence tools available, but also understand different means of presenting information based on its content, meaning, and what the audience needs.

What are organizational data teams?

Data teams are entities within an organization that provide both the leadership for and the execution of data governance. The data teams largely drive the culture and create the guidance that makes data governance work.

The types of data teams, their size, and membership will vary depending on the size and complexity of the organization itself. There are some general guidelines for the data teams an organization needs. A large organization may have a Chief Data Officer, whereas a smaller organization may incorporate those duties into another executive's role. An organization where most of its IT development work is performed in-house will need different types of technical and business data experts than one where IT is heavily invested in a Software as a Service model.

A Steering Committee will have the senior-most level of knowledge of the data governance program and is ultimately responsible for its success.

The data policies may be developed at this level. The committee is supported by a data governance office or administrator, who manages the overall program. The officer or administrator then communicates the program components to other data governance working teams within the organization. The steering committee must keep a constant eye on the organization's data governance status so they can identify and adapt to shortcomings and opportunities for improvement.

Leadership is also provided by the Data Governance Council, which is made up of ideally 3 to 5 chief stakeholders within the organization that hold key leadership responsibilities. The Data Governance Council sets priorities and is where the divisions work out how the Steering Committee's guidance will be put into practice. This is also where different disciplines can work together to reconcile what is desired out of data and business intelligence, and what constraints there are. The Council delegates responsibilities for different facets of data governance to its members for execution and implementation.

Building data governance is new and ongoing work that the Council has to do together. The Council, for example, determines what types of business intelligence are considered proprietary or what customer data elements are private personal information. These determinations apply to all areas of the organization regardless of whether or not they collect the data themselves, and what they are doing with it.

Depending on the organization's exact structure, the Steering Committee and the Data Governance Council may vary as to which is higher in the overall hierarchy, or whether they are co-equal partners.

We once saw a stark example of why this kind of universal oversight by the Data Governance Council is important. An organization's social media account was hacked and taken over, resulting in the exposure of a lot of member information to bad actors. The organization had to do extensive damage control with their members and work with them to identify tools to protect themselves. When we worked with them to determine how the account was hacked, it came up that a former employee still had administrative rights to the social media account. This individual had been hacked, which then allowed the attackers to gain control of the organization's account.

The organization had strong policies, processes, and procedures to ensure access to IT systems was revoked when an employee left. However, the social media account was not under direct IT management, so that guidance had never been extended to cover it. Finding and closing gaps like this is something that a cross-functional Data Governance Council does.

Data Governance Working Teams are involved at the tactical level, where data crosses business functions. These teams are very focused on specific issues or interactions between different functions, as opposed to working at a global level. These teams are more fluid, designed to adapt as the organization's goals, structure, and processes evolve. Members of these teams often include subject matter experts on organizational or divisional data that have extensive experience working with large bodies of data. Two other very important members are domain data stewards and data steward coordinators. Domain data stewards are experts on the organization's data hierarchy, the data dictionaries and glossaries, and similar resources. The data steward coordinators work with the data stewards at the operational level to ensure that the processes and procedures used within different business functions are consistent across the organization and support the overall data needs and business intelligence goals.

This may sound very technical, but the Data Governance Working Teams must include the business as well. While the domain stewards are part of IT, the subject matter experts are part of the business. They are the ones who know what the data means. IT and business are both represented on the working teams to ensure the data can be used to provide valuable business intelligence.

Finally, at the operational level are the business and technical data stewards. Data stewards are responsible for controlling the quality of the organization's data at all points of the information chain, from the point where it comes into the ecosphere all the way through to finished business intelligence products. At every stage, a business and a technical data steward should be working together to make sure data maintains acceptable quality and relevance for business intelligence. The business data stewards also partner with business stakeholders at different steps, particularly around data sources, data warehouses, and the business intelligence process to provide liaison between the business and IT.

Cultivating Talent

There are several challenges to an organization in cultivating a good data talent pool. A good part of it has been the shift away from data governance being primarily an IT responsibility. Many organizations may not recognize the need for business-side data expertise. For the business to give context and meaning to data and to help develop the necessary guidance, business units require people with a well-developed understanding of what data really is and how it works.

As business tools and Software as a Service move a lot of data collection and handling tools out of the direct control of an organization's IT, the business may even need to take on more direct responsibilities in ensuring data quality, privacy, and security.

Data-centered or data-heavy roles should be filled by people with existing data skills or relevant education and experience. If the word "data" is in the job title, the need for data expertise is obvious. If the need for data literacy or proficiency is only in a few bullets in the job description, the need for a candidate to have these skills or related competencies could easily be overlooked.

If the organization doesn't already have data experts in key positions, they can either create new roles and recruit people with the necessary skills or build up the skills of their existing employees. Giving business employees more technical knowledge of data tools and systems or increasing the overall data literacy throughout IT can foster the kind of collaboration and cooperation needed for data governance.

Taking courses à la carte or pursuing professional certifications might be all that's needed to round out an existing employee with the data literacy or technical skills to be a proper data caretaker for their role. The organization could pay for or subsidize this education or provide incentives to employees who pursue it on their own. Many schools and organizations provide training classes for organizations or offer group pricing for employees to take more targeted courses of study.

Even more informal types of talent development can work. With good data governance, there may be projects or initiatives where subject matter experts need to join the team, or somebody may need to cross-train with another area. Find employees who are eager to learn or have some core competencies or skills that they can use and get them on these teams. Give them a deeper dive into the data they work with and see if they can grow into more interesting and challenging roles.

Cultivating talent is about much more than just putting the right person in the seat. Data experts will still need to keep developing their skills and knowledge through continuing education, professional organization membership, mentorship within the organization, and knowledge-sharing with peers outside of it. The capabilities of business intelligence tools are continually evolving, so the experts taking care of the data going into them have to keep up. It's not enough to hire great people who can do amazing things with today's data and business intelligence tools and then let those skills stagnate as the world keeps moving forward.

An organization's data teams—especially at the strategic and executive levels—are composed primarily of people whose expertise is probably not rooted in data work, and yet they are tasked with providing vision and leadership for the organization's data efforts. These people do not need to become instant data professionals, but the more they understand data, the better leadership they can provide.

Who is creating your business intelligence?

Good business intelligence truly is a group effort. No one entity within an organization is responsible for putting quality reports and forecasts in front of decision makers. Nor is it simply a matter of IT creating a body of good data and then the business mining it for insights and meaning.

To get the best business intelligence, the organization must identify its body of data experts, the people involved at every stage of the process, from initially collecting data through the dashboard being published. These experts reside in all parts of the organization. Any place that data comes from or moves through needs to have skilled, knowledgeable people in place to handle the data themselves, or to provide guidance and support to those that do. This talent needs to be flexible and supported, so they can keep pace with changes both inside and outside of the organization that affect their data and the intelligence that comes from it.

Even though everybody in the organization is a data caretaker, there are still teams who focus specifically on data governance. At all levels, from the executive stakeholders to data stewards working within individual business units, there need to be groups of people that understand data and business intelligence well enough to provide leadership, vision, and guidance for data governance. The data teams don't need to be made up exclusively of experts, but everybody on the teams should have enough data literacy to communicate with experts and make well-informed decisions where data is concerned.

When everybody in the organization—experts and non-experts alike—are data literate and working together, every link on the chain, from initial collection to display on the executive dashboard, remains strong.

CHAPTER 11

Becoming a Data Governance Champion

For decision makers seeking to build up the quality of their business intelligence, data governance can look like a daunting task. Each of the five buckets covered so far, plus the culture to tie them all together, represents a potentially major undertaking depending on how much of a grasp the organization already has on these subjects and available resources.

To be successful in implementing data governance and data culture, the organization is going to need people to champion the cause. Some of the people best positioned to be those champions are the very people we're writing this book for—the executives and senior leadership and the data managers.

> ## *Data Literacy for Senior Leaders*
> For senior leaders, data literacy means the ability to strengthen data collection points, analyze for patterns and novelties, and interpret the data according to strengths while recognizing the limitations.

The top-level decision makers are dependent on high-quality business intelligence. They need the large quantities of raw data distilled into human-readable reports and forecasts so they can monitor the current health and future course of the organization. Meanwhile the data managers are the ones overseeing the processes of collecting and using the data itself. Both audiences have not only a vested interest in ensuring the integrity and accuracy of the data, but also the organizational authority to make the necessary changes to make data governance work.

Even though data governance and culture start at the top, they both need to flow through the entire organization. When looking at how to bring data governance in, it's easiest to break down the process into more manageable steps that can be implemented and appreciated throughout the organization. While the culture is being built from the top, start looking for low-hanging fruit and quick wins—places where small changes can quickly produce tangible results. This will show the entire organization that data governance benefits everybody, and that implementing doesn't mean disrupting the whole organization.

A key point to remember is that this commitment to strong data governance from the executive level will greatly improve the quality of data going into the business intelligence tools and processes, resulting in more accurate and insightful products coming out of it.

Build the Data Culture

The most important part of implementing strong data governance will be building the data culture to support and promote it. The whole organization is going to be affected by the work that's required. Processes and procedures need to be reviewed and revised. In many cases, new guidance needs to be developed, people need to be trained and mentored, and new standards will be implemented. Building data literacy within the organization requires learning a new vocabulary. People who didn't think they were handling data in the past must be aware that they are, and they need to take extra steps in their jobs to protect its integrity and accuracy.

The increase in work alone is a lot to ask of the organization's employees. Data governance also means sharing data across the organization. Business units need to trust each other and collaborate in ways they may not be accustomed to. We worked with one organization that didn't have a good sense of trust, so data and information was not reliably shared between business units. This resulted in a single event sponsorship being sold to one donor, and then a second one the next day. By not recognizing event sponsorship as valuable data that needed to be maintained and available to multiple departments, the organization ended up in the embarrassing position of having to cancel one of the sales.

Another place where trust comes in is if the organization has developed "shadow IT" in the process of implementing business technology without direct IT involvement. A strong working relationship between IT and the business must be in place to make sure data technology isn't being implemented piecemeal throughout the organization. This likely represents a big culture shift for the organization, and a major change in its mindset.

To accomplish good governance the organization needs to see that all of the leadership—from area supervisors to managers to senior leadership to executives—are fully committed to the effort. Data governance cannot take the form of a steady stream of directives and initiatives coming from above. This will quickly foster a feeling that data governance is being imposed upon the organization, which can easily lead to resistance to change.

Instead, leadership needs to show they are engaged and excited. They need to communicate that they understand all of this is new and it does come with extra responsibilities, but that there is a payoff at the end. Good data governance will help the organization to run more efficiently and to grow. As covered in the Data Culture chapter, employees who are asked to take on additional responsibilities to care for the data need to know that their leaders recognize this and actively support them.

Part of building the data culture initially will be defining the intelligence and data goals in terms that are real to the organization's employees. More growth can translate into more opportunities for advancement. Developing standard procedures for data handling across the organization means less tedious busy work manually cleaning up spreadsheets and more time doing meaningful and rewarding work. Collaboration across business units can be very exciting and round out people's skills, giving them more mobility within the organization to take their career in directions they never thought of before. It is important for leaders to find ways to highlight the tangible and intangible benefits of data governance.

Another key part of building the culture is for the leaders to lead by example by becoming more data literate themselves. Being able to speak confidently about what the data means and how it can be used, and to ask insightful questions when looking at business intelligence can increase people's confidence and engagement in their work. When leaders can clearly define what they need, and then provide feedback that shows they understand and appreciate the effort to meet those needs, the employees will feel more invested.

First Improvements

While building the data culture, work on building the infrastructure and practices for data governance as well. The organization doesn't need to wait until people are fully invested and dedicated to the effort before getting to work and showing results.

One thing that will drive adoption of data governance is demonstrating in realistic terms the types of effort that will be involved, and the return on that investment. One of the early stages of defining the organization's data ecology is to do an inventory of what data is being collected and handled, and where it is being stored. This will often reveal that there is duplicate data in the system, either because multiple business units are collecting similar information and not sharing it, or it is being accidentally duplicated while being communicated between systems or processed.

Setting up a process to clean up this duplicate data does several things. First, it shows that there might be duplication of effort going on, sometimes with people undoing each other's work. Hard numbers on how much duplicate or incorrect data is getting into the system can be available. Second, once the cleanup is in progress, the results of the cleaner, leaner data should be visible in the resulting business intelligence.

Another place to show some early results would be reviews of data handling procedures. This may not show the kind of immediate, easily quantifiable improvement that a data cleanup will, but it will show how many people in the organization handle data and highlight the importance of data stewardship. Developing common standards, processes, and procedures will encourage different business units to work together towards a clear common goal.

What are the goals?

Defining what the organization wants to get out of their data and business intelligence sets a target for everything that follows. Without clear goals in mind, moreover, strategy is going to be poorly defined, and the subsequent guidance will lack coherence. All of this will make it harder to create a good data culture.

The good news is that many organizations already have some sense of what their goals are. They need business intelligence to do things like support data-driven decision making, increase efficiency, protect member and organizational data, grow the organization, and predict and quickly adapt to emerging trends and technologies. There's a general "gut" feel that the organization wants to get some of the Big Data benefits that big commercial enterprises get.

There is another set of goals for data governance that looks beyond the business intelligence output, though. Data governance goals can also include increasing organizational data literacy, as well as training and mentoring staff in handling and using data, building standardized and repeatable processes, and increasing collaboration within the organization where data or business intelligence is concerned.

Once these goals are identified and stated, they need to be prioritized. Organizations will differ on how this is done. Where some may go for the low hanging fruit first, taking some quick wins where the goals are already close to being met to build confidence, others may see risks that need to be mitigated before expanding the capacity to collect and use data.

Data governance goals will be stable over time because they focus primarily on what the organization wants to accomplish over the long term.

Developing the Strategy

Once the end goals have been established, a strategy to build data governance that will support the goals needs to be developed. Strategy provides the guiding vision for how the goals will be accomplished. It is not dictating the specific actions to be taken, rather it helps set targets for the overall data governance effort.

When it's first implemented, the data governance strategy will be focused on developing the technology, guidance, and talent needed. Over time, the strategy will evolve to address maintenance of existing governance and keeping it strong.

While the strategy is similar to data governance goals, in that both are high-level guidance for the organization, strategy needs to be reviewed regularly to help the organization keep up with changing times. An annual review should be the bare minimum, if not biannually or even quarterly. There are always shifts in available technology, regulations and external standards, and market trends that will affect data governance strategy. Even organization size or an evolving membership base can necessitate changes to the strategy. For example, if the organization grows to the point where in-house data storage is becoming increasingly expensive, part of the data governance may be to shift to a cloud-based applications.

Some key elements of data governance strategy include data sources, tools, staffing, training, socialization, and data security and protection.

The tools to implement the strategy will come from both within and outside of the organization. Internal talent can be trained up and cross-functional workgroups can be established, as well as acquiring new software, looking at cloud storage, or seeking expert advice. A good place to start in developing the initial strategy is to look at the five buckets we've covered so far and see what the organization already has and what it needs in each of those realms. As an example, if there is no single location where the data policies, standards, processes, and procedures can be found, part of the strategy might direct the COO's office to consolidate and maintain all those materials in a master repository. Note that the strategy doesn't need to be granular down to what tool to house the guidance in and what staff needs to be added. It just places the responsibility on the COO to figure out how to do it. One aspect of the strategy that cannot be overlooked is the need to budget for data governance implementation. People are going to need resources—equipment, training, time, headcount—to make data governance work. No amount of culture building will get data governance off the ground if it is perceived as a series of unfunded mandates.

Create the Data Policies, Standards, Processes, and Procedures to Support the Strategy

Here is where the real work of making data governance happens. The data policies, standards, processes, and procedures bucket identifies four levels of policy, standard, process, and procedure to ensure a uniformity of effort and practice throughout the organization.

When formalizing data governance, taking a top-down approach to these steps will help a lot in structuring the effort, to make the whole process more efficient and minimize the duplication of work. The fortunate thing is that a lot of the guidance may already exist, just not within a single repository or with a clean line drawn from individual operational procedures up through a process to a standard and policy.

The first two steps of championing data governance can feed directly into developing the policies. The policies represent the organization's ultimate goals for their data governance efforts and the strategy determines what will be done at a high level to realize the goals. If a goal is to use business intelligence to grow membership, and a supporting strategy is to leverage demographic data collected via social media engagement, organizations need to ask what data policies will support the use of these data. Are there policies in place that ensure compliance with ethical standards and regulations when member data is collected and handled? Is there a policy that addresses security of third-party applications that are integrated with the rest of the data ecosphere? Are there data standards that ensure data coming in from a third-party business tool is compatible with data collected or generated by in-house applications managed by IT?

There is going to be an overlap when looking at goals, strategies, policies, and standards. In the example above, some of the policies and standards will apply to many, if not all, third-party applications or other tools that are not owned and managed directly by IT. When developing data governance guidance, look for these commonalities. Not only will it be more efficient to create a single, unified set of policies and standards to govern similar tools and applications, but it will also result in a simpler and more consistent body of guidance that is easier for the organization to adopt and adhere to.

Once the policies and standards are aligned with the goals and strategy, it's time to look at the existing body of processes and procedures. Just as with the policies and standards, make sure that processes and procedures that address similar tools or data types or operations are as consistent with each other as possible. Returning to the example above, because of the ethical and regulatory requirements around customer data, all processes or procedures around collecting and handling this data must comply with the same standards. IT, marketing, and billing can't each have their own guidance on what data can be shared and with whom. The social media managers and the database administrators are all part of the organization's human firewall, so they all require the same training on data privacy and security.

Seeing the Payoff

To achieve the full benefit of business intelligence, the entire organization will need to embrace data governance and its core principles. This is not going to be a quick process, but it can be relatively painless if it is done with intention and planning.

Many organizations are likely to have similar data governance goals—increase collaboration, protect, and secure data, ensure data complies with external standards and regulations—to get all of the organization's data tools and systems to work together.

Where business intelligence really enters into the data governance implementation is in the strategy. If a goal is to find ways to increase member engagement and retention, what sorts of data are needed to track and forecast these measures? If a goal is to bring new and more powerful business intelligence tools into the organization, the strategy may be to shift from in-house to cloud storage to maximize availability of data. A related strategy will be to develop more robust data privacy standards to account for this increase in the number of business units and systems that will be involved.

The executive, senior leaders, and data managers need to be vocal advocates of data governance throughout the process of developing goals and strategy, because they are asking a lot of the organization. The more effectively top leaders champion a data culture, the less resistance they are likely to face, and the easier it will be to start making the meaningful changes that affect the way people do their jobs. The leaders need to let everybody know how important good intelligence is to them in their decision making.

When the guidance starts being implemented at the operational level, better data will start coming into the ecosphere, resulting in better business intelligence being available. At this stage, championing data governance is going to mean talking about the increased accuracy and reliability of the intelligence products. Celebrate the wins, give credit where it is due. If part of the data governance strategy is to foster collaboration between business units, or have the business and IT create a comprehensive data dictionary, publicize it. Make sure the whole organization recognizes that their hard work and flexibility has turned into something measurable and real.

Appendix for Additional Resources and Tools

Business Intelligence Tools by Type of Use and Organizational Capacity

This is a way to think about your organization's capacity for using business intelligence tools (x-axis) business intelligence needs (y-axis) and some of the BI tools available on the market today. This diagram offers some guidance on how to interpret the information.

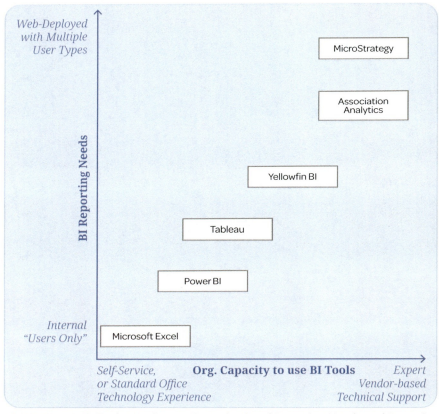

FIGURE 2 *How BI Tools Match up to Organizational Reporting Needs and Capacity.*

The lower left corner illustrates a BI tool that almost all organizations have at their disposal: Microsoft Excel. Excel can create charts and graphs and, with some additional training, can even provide a dashboard where data can be routinely updated and displayed.

In the lower middle are two tools in wide use: *Power BI* from Microsoft and *Tableau* from Salesforce. Both tools provide organizations with self-service options with some training for proficiency. Power BI makes use of Excel features, but stores the data securely and can create cloud-based dashboards for company use. Tableau goes further on the different user-type accessibility and visualization options. Both can link to multiple data sources. Tableau does come with a higher subscription price than Power BI if the organization is already a Microsoft 365 customer.

The top right corner describes three tools that are high-end and bring high value because they can handle large amounts of data in real time. They typically require expert technical skills to link operational and data warehouse storage areas. All of these come with subscription pricing.

This list of BI tools is *not* exhaustive. New products and features of current products are constantly being developed and we maintain and update our lists frequently. Please ask for more information.

Resources

This topic is rapidly changing and maturing as businesses understand their needs and goals. Here are just a few of the key resources used to guide the development of this book.

Books

These are three essential resources for data management and governance concepts:

DAMA International. (2017). *The Data Management Body of Knowledge (DAMA-DMBOK2)*. Technics Publications. ISBN-10: 1634622340

Algmin, Anthony J. (2019). *Data Leadership: Stop Talking about Data and Start Making an Impact*. DATAVERSITY Education LLC. ASIN: B07Z2K1D1B

Seiner, Robert. (2014). *Non-Invasive Data Governance: The Path of Least Resistance and Greatest Success*. Technics Publications. ASIN: B00N3259RG

Technical Whitepapers

Dedić, N., and Stanier, C. (2016). *Measuring the Success of Changes to Existing Business Intelligence Solutions to Improve Business Intelligence Reporting*. In: Tjoa, A., Xu, L., Raffai, M., Novak, N. (eds) *Research and Practical Issues of Enterprise Information Systems*. CONFENIS 2016. Lecture Notes in Business Information Processing, vol 268. Springer, Cham.
https://doi.org/10.1007/978-3-319-49944-4_17

Reinitz, B. (2019, Sept. 6). *Keys to an Analytics Future: Governance, Collaboration, and Communication*. Educause Blog.
https://er.educause.edu/blogs/2019/9/keys-to-an-analytics-future-governance-collaboration-and-communication

Simon, J., and Hubbard, D. (2019, August 12). *10 Best Practices to Ensure Data-Governance Efforts will Fail, Plus 10 Best Practices for Success*. Educause Blog.
https://er.educause.edu/articles/2019/8/10-best-practices-to-ensure-data-governance-efforts-will-fail-plus-10-best-practices-for-success

Resource Sites

DataVersity
https://www.dataversity.net

Domo
https://www.domo.com

Educause Data Governance Site
https://library.educause.edu/topics/administrative-and-business-services/data-governance

Gartner
https://www.gartner.com/en/insights

Business Intelligence (BI) Vendor Resources

Talend, The Definitive Guide to Data Governance
https://www.talend.com/resources/definitive-guide-data-governance

About the Authors

Daniel Elacqua is an experienced technology leader and certified Project Management Professional (PMP)® who has worked with non-profits and associations for more than 20 years. With a background in technology strategy, organizational strategy, IT governance, portfolio management, and project management, Daniel can take a holistic approach to data governance that is invaluable in fostering successful outcomes for his clients.

Prior to Strategico Consultants, Daniel worked at organizations such as the American Medical Informatics Association, Hartman Executive Advisors, NAFSA: Association of International Educators, Morpheus Project Consultants, and the American Specialty Toy Retailing Association (ASTRA). The breadth and depth of his experience gives him unique perspectives on the business needs of nonprofits and associations.

Gwen E. Garrison is a research and data strategist with a focus on data collection, reporting, and policies. With nearly 35 years of experience, building and sustaining organizational data use for critical policy and operational decision, she helps leverage organizational data assets through the trifecta of data skills: visualization, management, and governance. She has also managed large data systems with millions of records and thousands of variables with high ethical standards for privacy and security.

Dr. Garrison is the founder and principal data strategist at High Sierra Insights, where she and her team provide data governance, business intelligence, and evaluation services. She is also the founding director of Claremont Graduate University's Educational Evaluation and Data Analysis program and Clinical Full Professor in the School of Educational Studies. She has authored over 65 association- and academic-level publications and presentations.